はじめての
TOEFL Primary® テスト
問題集

監修●Global Communication & Testing

Step 1

くもん出版

監修のことば

　英語力に対する社会的な関心と要求が高まるなかで，子どもたちの英語学習開始年齢は年々低くなっています。しかしながら，低年齢層の英語学習に莫大な時間と費用が注がれている反面，その成果を確認・評価するためのグローバルスタンダードの英語テストが整っていませんでした。こうした状況に対し，世界最大のテスト開発機関であるEducational Testing Service（ETS）が，TOEFL Junior®に続いて初級英語学習者を対象に開発したのがTOEFL Primary®です。

　TOEFL Primary®では，小学生，中学生の日常生活での英語のコミュニケーションや，学校の授業や教科書など，親しみのあるシチュエーションの問題が出題されます。初期段階からグローバルスタンダードのTOEFL Primary®を受験し，英語学習の目標を持つことで「自分の英語がどの程度世界で通用するか」を客観的に評価できます。また上位テストであるTOEFL Junior®やTOEFL iBT®にも繋がり，将来の進路選択や職業選択の上でも役立ちます。

　本書はTOEFL Primary®を正しく理解いただき，受験される方々が受験前あるいは受験後に学習するために開発された参考書です。TOEFL Primary®のリーディング，リスニングそれぞれの試験形式を詳細に分析し，それらをレッスン別に紹介することにより，受験者の実力が十分に発揮できるよう配慮されています。また問題形式に十分に慣れていただけるよう，練習問題やミニテスト，実際の試験形式に即した模擬テスト（2回分）を用意しています。

　TOEFL Primary®受験の準備に加え，これから英語学習を深めていく方にとって，オーセンティックな（本物の）英語に触れていただける絶好の機会としてもご活用いただけます。

　TOEFL Primary®により現在の英語力を客観的に評価し，さらに英語力を伸ばそうと努力する子どもたちの一助として，本書が活用されることを願っています。

2015年2月
グローバル・コミュニケーション&テスティング

Contents
もくじ

Reading

Part 1

Unit 1 Picture Word Descriptions　（絵を見て読んで答えよう〈単語〉）

Lesson 1	What is your name?	**14**
Lesson 2	How are you?	**20**

Unit 2 Picture Sentence Descriptions　（絵を見て読んで答えよう〈文〉）

Lesson 3	What is she doing?	**28**
Lesson 4	Which is bigger?	**34**

Part 2

Unit 3 Word Riddles　（なぞなぞ）

Lesson 5	What is it?	**42**
Lesson 6	How does it look?	**48**

Part 3

Unit 4 Various Forms　（いろいろな文）

Lesson 7	When is the event?	**56**

Unit 5 Short Passages　（短い文章）

Lesson 8	What is the letter about?	**66**

Listening

Part 1

Unit 6 **Picture Descriptions** （絵を見て聞いて答えよう〈状態〉）

    Lesson 9   What is on the desk?   74

Part 2

Unit 7 **Instructions** （絵を見て聞いて答えよう〈指示〉）

    Lesson 10   What did she say?   84

Part 3

Unit 8 **Short Conversations** （短い会話）

    Lesson 11   Can you help me?   94
    Lesson 12   How are you feeling?   102

Part 4

Unit 9 **Long Conversations** （長い会話）

    Lesson 13   What does he want?   112
    Lesson 14   What will she do next?   120

Part 5

Unit 10 **Short Messages** （短いメッセージ）

    Lesson 15   Why did he call?   130
    Lesson 16   What is he talking about?   138

模擬テスト（2回分）   146
ワークブック   221
別冊 解答・解説

❯ TOEFL Primary®の概要

■ TOEFL Primary®について

TOEFL Primary®は，ETSが開発した，総合的な英語力を世界基準で測定するTOEFL®ファミリー最初のテストです。英語を母語としない小中学生を主な対象にデザインしており，アカデミックな英語と実用的な英語の両方の力を測定します。

TOEFL Primary®にはStep1とStep2の2段階のレベルのテストがあり，それぞれリーディングとリスニング能力を評価します。子どもでも取り組みやすい形式で，子どもの好奇心にこたえる内容の問題で構成されています。

■ テストの種類

1. リーディング・リスニングテスト - Step1

〈英語初級学習者を対象〉
身近な内容（学校，自宅，遊び場）
基本的な表現
日常的な物や人に関連する基本的な語彙および句
短く簡単な依頼文および指示文
日常体験に関する短く簡単な文章

2. リーディング・リスニングテスト - Step2

〈英語で多少のコミュニケーションをとることができる学習者を対象〉
基本的な表現，依頼文，指示文
日常体験のわくをこえる短く簡単なストーリーや会話
文脈上のヒントのある，少し難しい単語の含まれた文章
簡単な文章の読解

■ テストの分類

レベル	セクション	問題数	試験時間（分）	スコア	バンドスコア
Step 1	リーディング	39	約30分	100~109	1~4 (☆印で表示)
Step 1	リスニング	41	約30分	100~109	1~4 (☆印で表示)
Step 2	リーディング	37	約30分	100~115	1~5 (🏅で表示)
Step 2	リスニング	39	約30分	100~115	1~5 (🏅で表示)

リーディングのスコア

パフォーマンスの説明 (Performance Descriptors)	STEP 1	STEP 2
テスト内容を大変よく理解し運用できている。		🏅🏅🏅🏅🏅
簡単なストーリーや，年齢に合ったアカデミックな文章を理解している。		🏅🏅🏅🏅
Step 1: 短い説明や表示に記述されている情報，短いメッセージを理解している。 Step 2: 簡単なストーリーを理解し，年齢に合ったアカデミックな文章も理解し始めている。	☆☆☆☆	🏅🏅🏅
Step 1: 短い説明を理解し，表示や文章，予定表に書かれている情報を理解している。 Step 2: 短い説明を理解し，表示やメッセージ，ストーリーに記述されている情報を理解している。	☆☆☆	🏅🏅
単語や一部の短い説明を理解し始めている。	☆☆	
一部の基本的な単語を認識し始めている。	☆	🏅

リスニングのスコア

パフォーマンスの説明 (Performance Descriptors)	STEP 1	STEP 2
テスト内容を大変よく理解し運用できている。		🏅🏅🏅🏅🏅
会話や簡単なストーリー，年齢に合ったアカデミックな会話を理解している。		🏅🏅🏅🏅
Step 1: 簡単な説明や指示，会話，メッセージを理解している。 Step 2: 基本的な会話や簡単なストーリーを理解している。年齢に合ったアカデミックな会話も把握し始めている。	☆☆☆☆	🏅🏅🏅
Step 1: 短い簡単な説明や会話，メッセージを理解している。 Step 2: 基本的な会話やメッセージを理解し，ストーリーや情報の入った文章を把握し始めている。	☆☆☆	🏅🏅
話し言葉の一部の聞き覚えのある単語を認識し始めている。	☆☆	
話し言葉の物，場所，人など，聞き覚えのある単語を認識し始めている。	☆	🏅

TOEFL Primary®の特徴

1. 英語学習入門者のための評価試験

TOEFL Primary®は，満8歳から14歳の児童や生徒の情緒発達と認知能力に基づきアメリカで開発されたもので，児童や生徒の日常生活の経験にもとづいた内容を題材として取り入れています。さらに英語を母語としない小中学生を対象に行うテストとして，対象者の認知能力を考慮し，Step1には絵を多く取り入れ，小学校低学年でもアプローチしやすいように配慮されています。Step2においても，問題文，文章の長さ，難易度などが小中学生にふさわしいように設定されています。

2. ETSが開発した国際的な評価

世界的に認知されているETSが開発したTOEFL Primary®は，TOEFL®ファミリーを構成するTOEFL Junior®，TOEFL iBT®などとともに，学習者の英語力を全世界で比較することができるテストです。

3. Lexile®（レクサイル）指数との連携

Lexile®指数は，英文を読む力と英文の難易度のそれぞれを，統一的な尺度を用いて示すものです。TOEFL Primary®スコアレポートにおける「リーディング」項目では，Lexile®指数を記載しており，受験者が自分の読書力に合った英語の本を探す際の目安とすることができます。米国Metametrics社が開発したこのLexile®指数は，すでにTOEFL Junior®，TOEFL iBT®など主要なテストで広く活用されています。

4. CEFR

「Common European Framework of Reference for Languages（ヨーロッパ言語共通参照枠）」。欧州評議会（Council of Europe）によって2001年に「ヨーロッパの言語教育の向上のために基盤を作ること」を目標に公開された枠組みで，ABCの3段階をさらに2分割したA1、A2、B1、B2、C1、C2の合計6段階のレベルで言語力を表す評価基準です。
TOEFL Primary®のスコアレポートには試験のバンドスコアとともにCEFR基準によるバンドスコアが記載され，受験者の英語力を国際的な基準によって比較することができます。

■ TOEFL® ファミリーラインナップ

TOEFL Primary®の誕生により，ETSのTOEFL®テストは，対象者ごとに体系化された一連のテストを提供できるようになりました。英語入門段階の児童・生徒を対象としたTOEFL Primary®，中級段階の学生を対象とするTOEFL Junior®，そして上級段階のTOEFL iBT®と，英語学習者は小学生から成人に至るまで，ETSが実施する一貫した基準で，正確に自身の英語力を評価することができます。

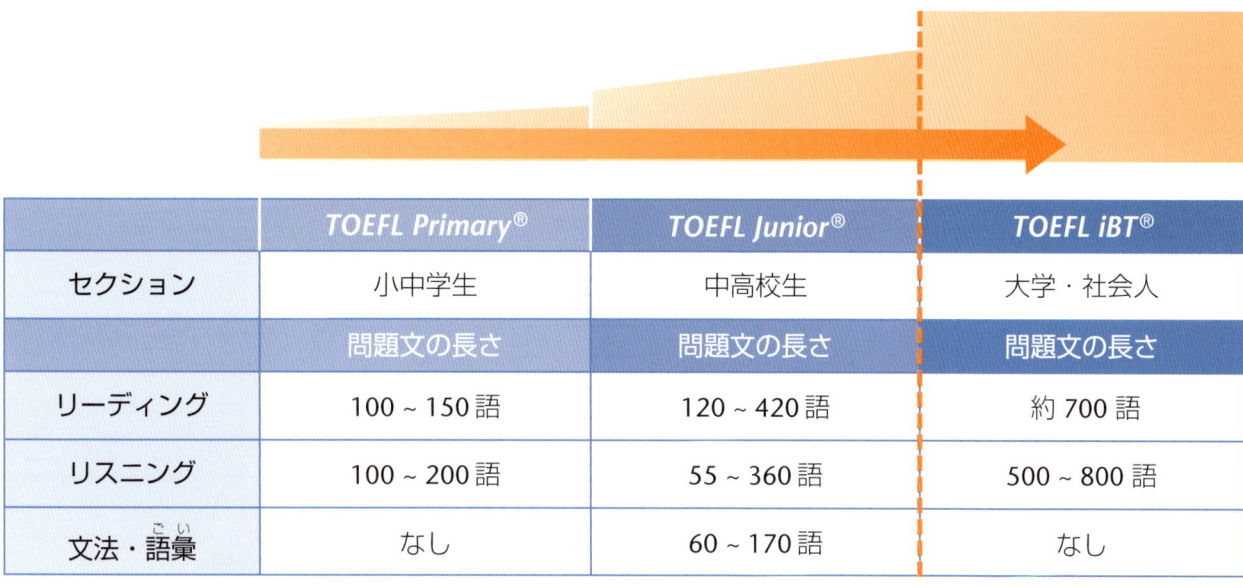

	TOEFL Primary®	TOEFL Junior®	TOEFL iBT®
セクション	小中学生	中高校生	大学・社会人
	問題文の長さ	問題文の長さ	問題文の長さ
リーディング	100～150語	120～420語	約700語
リスニング	100～200語	55～360語	500～800語
文法・語彙	なし	60～170語	なし

本書について

問題形式の説明と例題

- 問題形式を紹介し，各形式の例文を提示します。
- 問題を解くヒントとなる例題（Example）を示し，学習者が各形式に習熟できるようにしています。
- リーディングでは問題文のLexile®ガイド欄を設け，問題文のおおよその難度を予測できるようにしています。

Script …音声の内容
CDのナンバー
トラックナンバー

重要ポイント

- 各レッスンでは学習する文法（リーディング）と表現（リスニング）を例文とともに提示し，重要な文法事項や表現を自然に習得できるようにしています。

練習問題

- 学習した問題形式に対応した練習問題を収録しています。
- 形式ごとに問題を集中的に練習することで，各問題形式に習熟することができます。

Reading
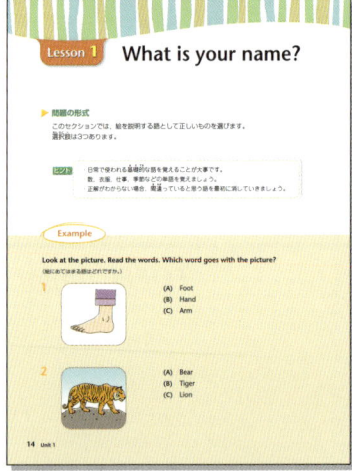
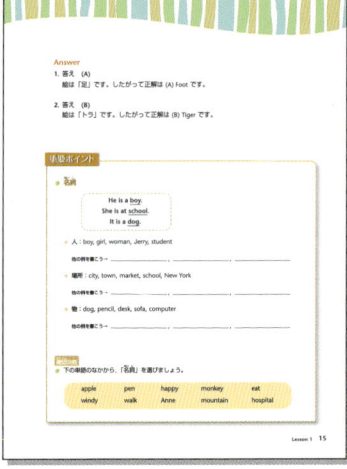
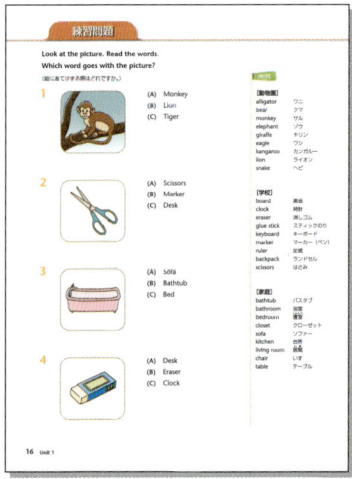

Listening

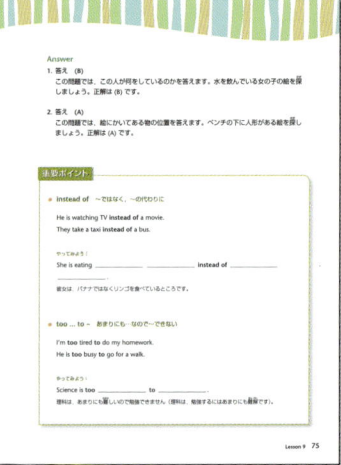
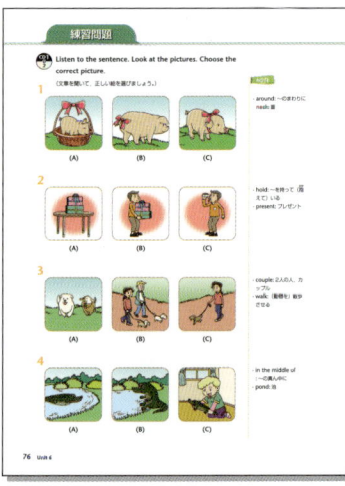

ミニテスト

- 実際のTOEFL Primary®テストにそった各形式の問題を収録しています。上段にはマークシート方式の解答用紙を掲載し，実践練習を積むことができます。

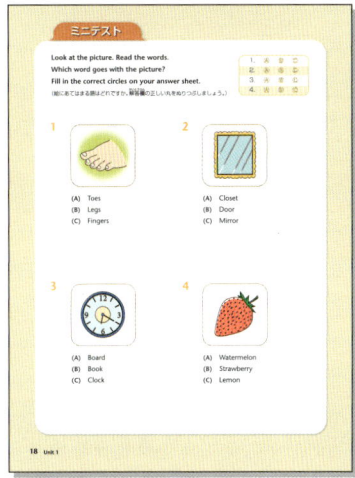

模擬テスト

- 実際のテストと同じ形式で出題されます。全2回分ありTOEFL Primary®テストの実践的な練習を十分に積むことができるようにしています。

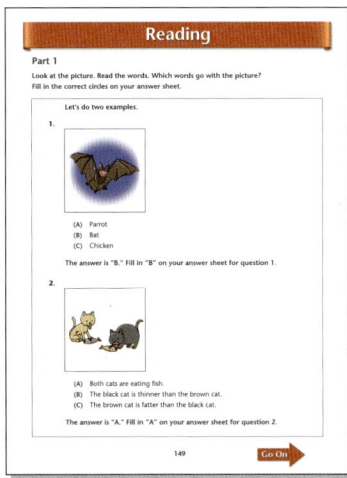

ワークブック

- Word List（単語帳）：各レッスンで学習した重要単語をリストにして掲載しています。
- Word Study（単語学習）：リストに掲載した単語を，簡単な問題を通じて復習することができます。
- Chunk Study（フレーズ学習）：単語以外の熟語表現を文章とともに練習することができます。

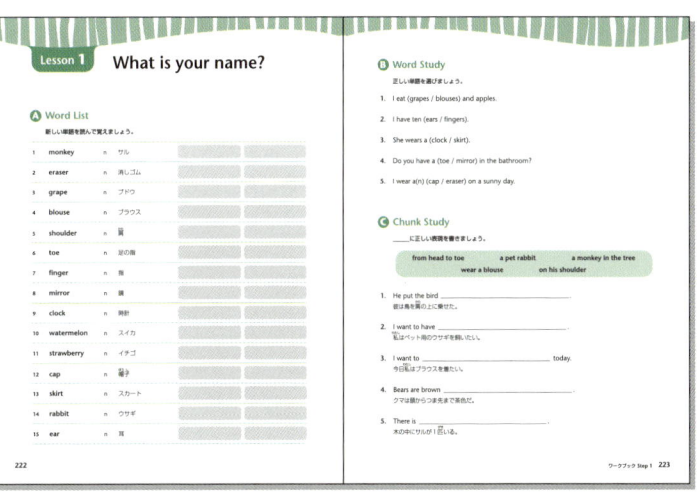

11

Reading
Part 1

Unit 1

Picture Word Descriptions
(絵を見て読んで答えよう〈単語〉)

> Lesson 1   What is your name?
> Lesson 2   How are you?

Lesson 1 What is your name?

▶ 問題の形式

このセクションでは，絵を説明する語として正しいものを選びます。
選択肢は3つあります。

> ヒント
> ・日常で使われる基礎的な語を覚えることが大事です。
> ・数，衣服，仕事，季節などの単語を覚えましょう。
> ・正解がわからない場合，間違っていると思う語を最初に外していきましょう。

Example

Look at the picture. Read the words. Which word goes with the picture?
（絵にあてはまる語はどれですか。）

1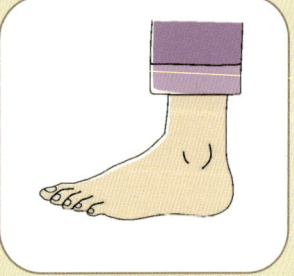

(A) Foot
(B) Hand
(C) Arm

2

(A) Bear
(B) Tiger
(C) Lion

Answer

1. 答え　(A)

    絵は「足」です。したがって正解は (A) Foot です。

2. 答え　(B)

    絵は「トラ」です。したがって正解は (B) Tiger です。

重要ポイント

名詞

> He is a <u>boy</u>.
> She is at <u>school</u>.
> It is a <u>dog</u>.

人：boy, girl, woman, Jerry, student

他の例を書こう→ _____ , _____ , _____

場所：city, town, market, school, New York

他の例を書こう→ _____ , _____ , _____

物：dog, pencil, desk, sofa, computer

他の例を書こう→ _____ , _____ , _____

確認問題

下の単語のなかから，「名詞」を選びましょう。

| apple | pen | happy | monkey | eat |
| windy | walk | Anne | mountain | hospital |

練習問題

Look at the picture. Read the words.
Which word goes with the picture?
(絵にあてはまる語はどれですか。)

NOTE

1
- (A) Monkey
- (B) Lion
- (C) Tiger

[動物園]

alligator	ワニ
bear	クマ
monkey	サル
elephant	ゾウ
giraffe	キリン
eagle	ワシ
kangaroo	カンガルー
lion	ライオン
snake	ヘビ

2
- (A) Scissors
- (B) Marker
- (C) Desk

[学校]

board	黒板
clock	時計
eraser	消しゴム
glue stick	スティックのり
keyboard	キーボード
marker	マーカー（ペン）
ruler	定規
backpack	ランドセル
scissors	はさみ

3
- (A) Sofa
- (B) Bathtub
- (C) Bed

[家庭]

bathtub	バスタブ
bathroom	浴室
bedroom	寝室
closet	クローゼット
sofa	ソファー
kitchen	台所
living room	居間
chair	いす
table	テーブル

4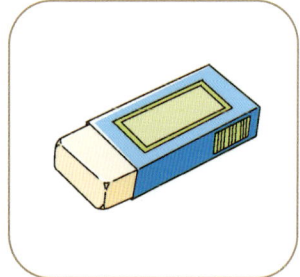
- (A) Desk
- (B) Eraser
- (C) Clock

5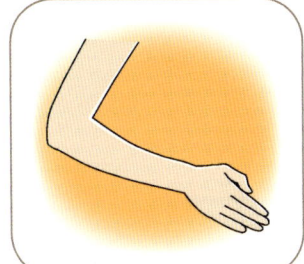
- (A) Arm
- (B) Leg
- (C) Face

6
- (A) Grape
- (B) Banana
- (C) Peach

7
- (A) Glove
- (B) Shirt
- (C) Blouse

8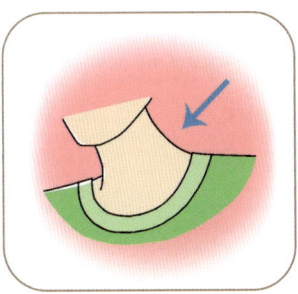
- (A) Shoulder
- (B) Back
- (C) Neck

NOTE

[人体]

arm	腕
back	背中
face	顔
finger	指
foot	足
leg	脚
neck	首
shoulder	肩
toe	足の指

[果物]

apple	リンゴ
cherry	サクランボ
grape	ブドウ
watermelon	スイカ
strawberry	イチゴ
orange	オレンジ
peach	モモ
pineapple	パイナップル
lemon	レモン

[衣服]

belt	ベルト
cap	帽子（キャップ）
coat	コート
glove	手袋
jacket	ジャケット（上着）
pants	パンツ（ズボン）
shirt	シャツ, 肌着
skirt	スカート
jeans	ジーンズ

ミニテスト

Look at the picture. Read the words.
Which word goes with the picture?
Fill in the correct circles on your answer sheet.
（絵にあてはまる語はどれですか。解答欄の正しい丸をぬりつぶしましょう。）

1.	Ⓐ	Ⓑ	Ⓒ
2.	Ⓐ	Ⓑ	Ⓒ
3.	Ⓐ	Ⓑ	Ⓒ
4.	Ⓐ	Ⓑ	Ⓒ

1

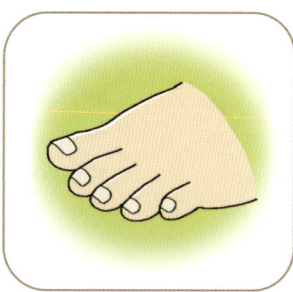

(A) Toes
(B) Legs
(C) Fingers

2

(A) Closet
(B) Door
(C) Mirror

3

(A) Board
(B) Book
(C) Clock

4

(A) Watermelon
(B) Strawberry
(C) Lemon

5.	Ⓐ	Ⓑ	Ⓒ
6.	Ⓐ	Ⓑ	Ⓒ
7.	Ⓐ	Ⓑ	Ⓒ
8.	Ⓐ	Ⓑ	Ⓒ

5

(A) Cap
(B) Jeans
(C) Skirt

6

(A) Cow
(B) Rabbit
(C) Pig

7

(A) Boots
(B) Sneakers
(C) Gloves

8

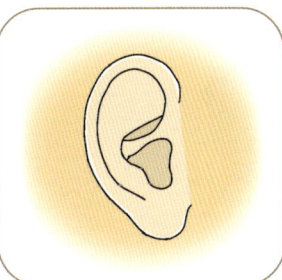

(A) Mouth
(B) Eye
(C) Ear

Lesson 2 How are you?

▶ **問題の形式**

このセクションでは，絵で表された行動や感情，特徴を最も正しく説明している単語を選びます。
選択肢は3つあります。

ヒント
・このセクションで使われる単語は難しいものではありません。人や物を表す基礎的な単語を覚えてください。
・正解がわからない場合，まず間違っている単語を外していきましょう。

Example

Look at the picture. Read the words. Which word goes with the picture?
（絵にあてはまる語はどれですか。）

1
  (A) Speak
  (B) Study
  (C) Send

2
  (A) Red umbrella
  (B) Blue umbrella
  (C) Yellow umbrella

Answer

1. 答え （B）
   絵の中の少年は本を読んでいます。したがって正解は (B) Study（学習する）です。

2. 答え （A）
   絵の中の傘の色は赤です。したがって正解は (A) Red umbrella（赤い傘）です。

重要ポイント

動詞

> I dance.
> I like bananas.

play, dance, clap, swim, brush, make, have, look, like, love, want, wish, hope

形容詞

> I am happy.
> It is blue.

感情：glad, happy, sad, scared, tired, surprised, worried

形：fat, big, small, short, thin

色：yellow, blue, red, brown, black, white

確認問題

単語を読んで，動詞には V，形容詞には A と書きましょう。

1. jump (　　)　　2. sad (　　)　　3. sleep (　　)　　4. green (　　)
5. windy (　　)　　6. touch (　　)　　7. eat (　　)　　8. slow (　　)

練習問題

**Look at the picture. Read the words.
Which word goes with the picture?**

（絵にあてはまる語はどれですか。）

1
 - (A) Talk
 - (B) Cry
 - (C) Smile

2
 - (A) Sing
 - (B) Learn
 - (C) Shake

3
 - (A) Run
 - (B) Paint
 - (C) Write

4
 - (A) Stop
 - (B) Stand
 - (C) Sit

NOTE

[動詞]
：動詞は，人や物の動きを表す語です。

cry	泣く
cut	切る
draw	描く
drink	飲む
help	助ける
laugh	笑う
learn	学ぶ
listen	聞く
look	見る
make	作る
open	開ける
run	走る
see	見える
shake	振る
sing	歌う
sit	座る
sleep	眠る
smell	においをかぐ
speak	話す
stand	立つ
stop	立ち止まる
think	考える
walk	歩く
wash	洗う
write	（字を）書く

5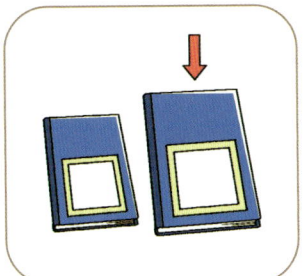
- (A) Small book
- (B) Big book
- (C) Old book

6
- (A) Cold water
- (B) Warm water
- (C) Hot water

7
- (A) Snowy
- (B) Cloudy
- (C) Rainy

8
- (A) Weak
- (B) Strong
- (C) Long

NOTE

[形容詞]
形容詞は，人の感情や性格，人や，物の性質，状態などを表す語です。

cloudy	くもった
cold	冷たい（寒い）
early	（時刻が）早い
fast	（速度が）速い
fat	太っている
happy	幸福な
hot	熱い（暑い）
large	大きい
late	（時刻が）遅い
left	左の
long	長い
old	年とっている，古い
rainy	雨降りの
right	右の
sad	悲しい
short	短い
slow	（速度が）遅い
small	小さい
snowy	雪の降る
strong	強い
sunny	日が照っている
thin	薄い
weak	弱い
windy	風が吹いている
young	若い

Lesson 2

ミニテスト

Look at the picture. Read the words.
Which words goes with the picture?
Fill in the correct circles on your answer sheet.
（絵にあてはまる語はどれですか。解答欄の正しい丸をぬりつぶしましょう。）

1.	Ⓐ	Ⓑ	Ⓒ
2.	Ⓐ	Ⓑ	Ⓒ
3.	Ⓐ	Ⓑ	Ⓒ
4.	Ⓐ	Ⓑ	Ⓒ

1

(A)　Start
(B)　Stand
(C)　Stop

2

(A)　Fast car
(B)　Fast train
(C)　Big plane

3

(A)　Eat
(B)　Help
(C)　Learn

4

(A)　Sunny
(B)　Dark
(C)　Bright

5.	Ⓐ	Ⓑ	Ⓒ
6.	Ⓐ	Ⓑ	Ⓒ
7.	Ⓐ	Ⓑ	Ⓒ
8.	Ⓐ	Ⓑ	Ⓒ

5

- (A) Drive
- (B) Make
- (C) Walk

6

- (A) Give
- (B) Take
- (C) Jump

7

- (A) Thin bear
- (B) Fat bear
- (C) Weak bear

8

- (A) Purple box
- (B) Round box
- (C) Brown box

Reading Part 1

Unit 2
Picture Sentence Descriptions
（絵を見て読んで答えよう〈文〉）

> Lesson 3　　What is she doing?

> Lesson 4　　Which is bigger?

Lesson 3 What is she doing?

▶ 問題の形式

このセクションでは、絵で表された行動や状況を最も正しく説明している文を選びます。選択肢は3つあります。

ヒント
- 文の中で「なにが」「だれが」などを表すものを「主語」といいます。このセクションでは、まず主語を見つけましょう。
- 文の主語が人である場合、男性なのか女性なのか、何人なのか考えましょう。
- 行われていることを見て、それがもう終わったことなのかどうか考えましょう。

Example

Look at the picture. Read the sentences. Which sentence goes with the picture?
(絵にあてはまる文はどれですか。)

1
- (A) The door is open.
- (B) Today is cloudy.
- (C) The window is open.

2
- (A) The man is cutting an apple.
- (B) The man is eating an apple.
- (C) There are many apples on the table.

Answer

1. 答え　(C)

絵では，窓が大きく開いていて太陽が照っています。したがって正解は (C) The window is open.（窓は開いています）です。

2. 答え　(A)

絵では，男の人がリンゴを半分に切っているところです。したがって正解は (A) The man is cutting an apple.（男の人がリンゴを切っています）です。

重要ポイント

● 時制

昨日	今日	今
I play*ed* the piano.	I **play** the piano.	I *am* play*ing* the piano.
I bake*d* cookies.	I **bake** cookies.	I *am* bak*ing* cookies.
I stud*ied* math.	I **study** math.	I *am* study*ing* math.
I plan*ned* the party.	I **plan** the party.	I *am* plan*ning* the party.

確認問題

● 正しい時制にして空欄をうめましょう。

昨日	今日	今
I watched TV.	1. _____	I am watching TV.
2. _____	I walk to school.	I am walking to school.
I talked to mom.	I talk to mom.	3. _____

Lesson 3　29

練習問題

Look at the picture. Read the sentences.
Which sentence goes with the picture?
（絵にあてはまる文はどれですか。）

NOTE

1
- (A) He is choosing bananas.
- (B) She is eating apples.
- (C) She is choosing apples.

· choose: 選ぶ

2
- (A) The girl is swimming with a dog.
- (B) The dog is running with a girl.
- (C) The girl is talking to a dog.

· swim: 泳ぐ
· run: 走る
· talk: 話す

3
- (A) The phone is ringing in the bedroom.
- (B) The alarm clock is ringing in the bedroom.
- (C) The alarm clock is ringing in the living room.

· phone: 電話
· ring: 鳴る
· alarm clock: 目覚まし時計

4
- (A) The boy and the girl are reading a book.
- (B) The boy is singing with the girl.
- (C) The girl reads a book and the boy sings a song.

· read: 読む
· sing: 歌う

5
(A) The cat is walking on the sofa.
(B) The cat is sleeping under the cushion.
(C) The cat is sleeping on the cushion.

- sofa: ソファー
- sleep: 眠る
- cushion: クッション

6
(A) The man is reading a book.
(B) The man is ordering food.
(C) The woman wants steak.

- order: 注文する
- steak: ステーキ

7
(A) She is waiting for a bus.
(B) He is taking a bus.
(C) He is waiting for a bus.

- wait: 待つ
- take a bus: バスに乗る

8
(A) The girl plays the drums.
(B) The girl is playing the keyboard.
(C) There are eight drums.

- play: 演奏する
- drum: ドラム
- keyboard: キーボード

Lesson 3   31

ミニテスト

Look at the picture. Read the sentences.
Which sentence goes with the picture?
Fill in the correct circles on your answer sheet.

（絵にあてはまる文はどれですか。解答欄の正しい丸をぬりつぶしましょう。）

1.	Ⓐ	Ⓑ	Ⓒ
2.	Ⓐ	Ⓑ	Ⓒ
3.	Ⓐ	Ⓑ	Ⓒ
4.	Ⓐ	Ⓑ	Ⓒ

1

(A)　She is wearing a blue sweater.
(B)　She is running in the street.
(C)　She is riding inline skates.

2

(A)　She is kicking a ball.
(B)　They are playing with a ball.
(C)　She catches a ball.

3

(A)　They are not hungry.
(B)　Two birds are in a nest.
(C)　Two birds are flying.

4

(A)　The giraffe's neck is long.
(B)　There are three legs.
(C)　The giraffe is running.

5

(A) The boy is holding popcorn.
(B) The boy is wearing a yellow shirt.
(C) The boy doesn't like cotton candy.

6

(A) He wants to drink water.
(B) He is cold.
(C) He is not thirsty.

7

(A) Yesterday was sunny and bright.
(B) There are many trees.
(C) The weather is very windy.

8

(A) Two books are under the desk.
(B) The girl is raising her hand high.
(C) The girl is sitting on the desk.

Lesson 4　Which is bigger?

▶ 問題の形式

このセクションでは，絵で示されているものを最もうまく説明している文を選びます。選択肢は3つあります。

> **ヒント**
> ・選択肢の文の主語を見つけましょう。そうすると，物や人を比較するのが楽になります。
> ・比較をしているものどうしの，類似点や相違点を見つけましょう。
> ・選択肢の文の主語が同じ場合，主語の後に続く語句を見て考えましょう。
> ・事前に，形容詞の比較級，最上級の形を勉強しておきましょう。

Example

Look at the picture. Read the sentences. Which sentence goes with the picture?
（絵にあてはまる文はどれですか。）

1
- (A) The dog is smaller than the cat.
- (B) The cat is smaller than the dog.
- (C) There are two dogs.

2
- (A) Two girls are walking together.
- (B) The girl in a blue shirt is faster than the other girl.
- (C) The girl in a yellow shirt is faster than the girl in a blue shirt.

Answer

1. 答え (B)

絵では，小さいネコが大きな犬のとなりに座っています。したがって正解は (B) The cat is smaller than the dog.（ネコは犬より小さい）です。

2. 答え (B)

絵では，2人の女の子が走っています。青いシャツの女の子が，黄色いシャツの女の子より前にいます。したがって正解は (B) The girl in a blue shirt is faster than the other girl.（青いシャツの女の子は，もう一人の女の子より足が速い）です。

重要ポイント

- **-er / -est**

    tall
    I am tall**er than** you.
    I am **the** tall**est** student in my class.

    pretty
    She is prett**ier than** me.
    She is **the** prett**iest** girl in this town.

- **as ~ as**

    slow
    I am **as slow as** my brother.

確認問題

正しい単語を選びましょう。

1. Turtles are (fast / faster) than snails.

2. He is (as richer as / as rich as) his friend.

3. She is (the smarter / the smartest) student in this class.

4. They are (as tall as / the tallest) their parents.

練習問題

Look at the picture. Read the sentences.
Which sentence goes with the picture?
（絵にあてはまる文はどれですか。）

NOTE

1

(A) Three pencils are on the desk.
(B) The red pencil is the longest one.
(C) The green pencil is longer than the yellow pencil.

· long - longer - longest
· pencil: 鉛筆
· red: 赤い
· green: 緑の
· yellow: 黄色い

2

(A) The pink shirt is larger than the green shirt.
(B) The pink shirt is as big as the green shirt.
(C) The pink shirt is smaller than the green shirt.

· large - larger - largest
· pink: ピンク色の
· shirt: シャツ, 肌着

3

(A) The girl in blue pants is as tall as the boy.
(B) The boy is the tallest student in the group.
(C) The girl in a yellow skirt is the shortest.

· tall - taller - tallest
· short - shorter - shortest
· blue: 青い
· skirt: スカート

4

(A) The brown gloves are bigger than the blue gloves.
(B) The blue gloves are cleaner than the brown gloves.
(C) The gloves have the same color.

· clean - cleaner - cleanest
· brown: 茶色い
· glove: 手袋

5

(A) The mouse is the heaviest animal in the group.
(B) The panda is heavier than the mouse.
(C) There are three monkeys in the picture.

NOTE

· heavy - heavier - heaviest

· mouse: ネズミ
· panda: パンダ
· monkey: サル

6

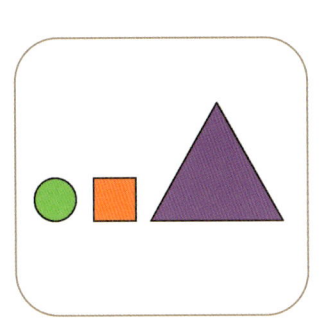

(A) The purple triangle and the orange square are the same size.
(B) The green circle is next to the purple triangle.
(C) The triangle is the biggest shape.

· big - bigger - biggest
· purple: 紫色の
· triangle: 三角形
· square: 正方形
· circle: 丸（円）

7

(A) The father is the tallest in the family.
(B) The baby is the youngest in the family.
(C) The boy is standing next to the mother.

· tall - taller - tallest
· young - younger - youngest

· family: 家族
· baby: 赤ちゃん
· next to: 〜のとなりに

8

(A) The house is in front of the tree.
(B) The tree is next to the house.
(C) The house is behind the tree.

· in front of: 〜の前に
· next to: 〜の横に
· behind: 〜の後ろに

ミニテスト

Look at the picture. Read the sentences.
Which sentence goes with the picture?
Fill in the correct circles on your answer sheet.
（絵にあてはまる文はどれですか。解答欄の正しい丸をぬりつぶしましょう。）

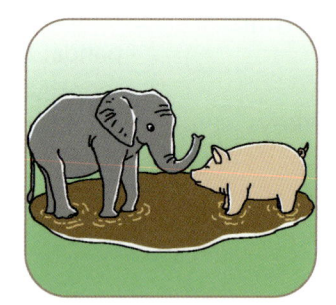

1.	Ⓐ	Ⓑ	Ⓒ
2.	Ⓐ	Ⓑ	Ⓒ
3.	Ⓐ	Ⓑ	Ⓒ
4.	Ⓐ	Ⓑ	Ⓒ

1

(A) Two pigs are playing in the pool.
(B) The elephant is larger than the pig.
(C) The pig and the elephant are the same size.

2

(A) The black paint can is bigger than the yellow paint can.
(B) Both are the same color.
(C) The yellow paint can is as big as the black paint can.

3

(A) The boy is younger than the girl.
(B) The girl is smaller than the boy.
(C) Both are very old.

4

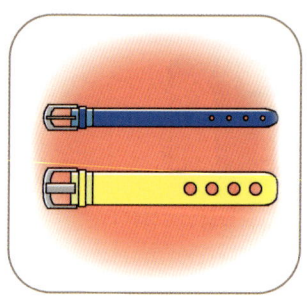

(A) Both belts have the same color.
(B) The yellow belt is wider than the blue belt.
(C) The blue belt is as wide as the yellow belt.

5.	Ⓐ	Ⓑ	Ⓒ
6.	Ⓐ	Ⓑ	Ⓒ
7.	Ⓐ	Ⓑ	Ⓒ
8.	Ⓐ	Ⓑ	Ⓒ

5

(A) The girl is happier than the boy.
(B) The boy and the girl are happy.
(C) The boy is happier than the girl.

6

(A) The green building is higher than the blue building.
(B) The orange building is the highest building.
(C) The blue building is as high as the orange building.

7

(A) There are two coats on the table.
(B) The coat is warmer than the blouse.
(C) The blouse is warmer than the coat.

8

(A) It was rainy yesterday.
(B) Yesterday was colder than today.
(C) Today is colder than yesterday.

Reading Part 2

Unit 3

Word Riddles
(なぞなぞ)

❯ Lesson 5   What is it?

❯ Lesson 6   How does it look?

Lesson 5 What is it?

▶ **問題の形式**

このセクションでは，人や物の名前について，2つから3つの説明文が提示されます。その説明文や質問にあてはまる単語を選びましょう。
選択肢は3つあります。

ヒント
- まずよく知っている語を探し，それがあてはまるかどうか考えます。
- あてはまらない語があれば，外しましょう。

Example

Read and find the answer.
（問題を読んで，答えを選びましょう。）

1. They cook food for you. They work in restaurants. They sometimes wear a white hat.
   They are _____.

   (A) chefs
   (B) nurses
   (C) astronauts

2. People buy things to read here. There are many shelves. It is usually quiet.
   What is it?

   (A) A bookstore
   (B) A cafeteria
   (C) A supermarket

Answer

1. 答え (A)

問題文では，レストランで，白い帽子をかぶって料理をする人の事が書かれています。したがって正解は (A) chefs（シェフ，コック）です。

2. 答え (A)

問題文では，読むための物を買い，本棚がたくさんあって，静かな場所だと説明されています。したがって正解は (A) A bookstore（本屋）です。

重要ポイント

a/an + 名詞

a	a star	a bus	a pencil	a boy
an	an hour	an image	an apple	an umbrella

a cat / two cats

-s	radio → radios, hat → hats, girl → girls
-es	box → boxes, tomato → tomatoes, dish → dishes
-y → -ies	lady → ladies, baby → babies, candy → candies
-f(e) → -ves	wife → wives, wolf → wolves, leaf → leaves

確認問題

それぞれの語の前に，**a**，**an**，**x**（なし）を入れてください。

1. _____ room
2. _____ apple
3. _____ bananas
4. _____ pencils
5. _____ car
6. _____ elephant
7. _____ picture
8. _____ wolves
9. _____ men

Lesson 5　43

練習問題

Read and find the answer.
（問題を読んで，答えを選びましょう。）

1 It swims in the sea. It has sharp teeth and fins.
It is a _____ .

- (A) frog
- (B) shark
- (C) squid

> **NOTE**
> ・sharp: するどい
> ・teeth: 歯
> 　（toothの複数形）
> ・fin: ヒレ

2 They work on farms. They grow vegetables for you.
They are strong.
Who are they?

- (A) Nurses
- (B) Farmers
- (C) Cows

> ・farm: 農場
> ・grow: 育てる

3 They are in movies. You also see them on TV. They make you laugh or cry.
Who are they?

- (A) Actors
- (B) Cooks
- (C) Teachers

> ・movie: 映画
> ・laugh: 笑う

4 It is sweet. It is usually brown. Sometimes it is dark and sometimes it is light.
What is it?

- (A) Cherry
- (B) Orange
- (C) Chocolate

> ・sweet: 甘い
> ・dark:（色が）暗い
> ・light:（色が）明るい

44　Unit 3

5 You play this. You use a racket. You hit a yellow ball. What is it?

- (A) Tennis
- (B) Baseball
- (C) Badminton

- racket: ラケット
- hit: 打つ

6 It is a type of sandwich. You can find meat and cheese on it.
What is it?

- (A) A burger
- (B) A pasta
- (C) A cookie

- type: 種類
- meat: 肉
- cheese: チーズ

7 This is a healthy food. It is a vegetable. Its color is orange. What is it?

- (A) A potato
- (B) A carrot
- (C) An apple

- healthy: 健康によい
- vegetable: 野菜

8 It is round. It comes in red, brown, and black. It is a food. What is it?

- (A) A bean
- (B) A ball
- (C) A watermelon

- round: まるい

ミニテスト

Read and find the answer.
Fill in the correct circles on your answer sheet.
（問題を読んで、答えを選びましょう。解答欄の正しい丸をぬりつぶしましょう。）

1. Ⓐ Ⓑ Ⓒ
2. Ⓐ Ⓑ Ⓒ
3. Ⓐ Ⓑ Ⓒ
4. Ⓐ Ⓑ Ⓒ

1 You can read books here. You study here. You must be very quiet. Where is it?

- (A) A living room
- (B) A store
- (C) A library

2 You turn older on this day. You have a party. All of your friends come. What is it?

- (A) A birthday
- (B) A holiday
- (C) A meeting

3 It is an animal. It lives by the sea. It has a round body and walks sideways. What is it?

- (A) An alligator
- (B) A shark
- (C) A crab

4 It is yellow. There are many little pieces on it. Sometimes you pop it for a snack. Sometimes you eat it on a stick. What is it?

- (A) Rice
- (B) Corn
- (C) Banana

5.	Ⓐ	Ⓑ	Ⓒ
6.	Ⓐ	Ⓑ	Ⓒ
7.	Ⓐ	Ⓑ	Ⓒ
8.	Ⓐ	Ⓑ	Ⓒ

5 It can be green, yellow or red. Sometimes it is very spicy.
It is a(n) _____ .

(A) pepper
(B) grape
(C) onion

6 You eat it. It is usually round and sweet. Sometimes it has chocolate chips in it.
What is it?

(A) A caramel
(B) A cake
(C) A cookie

7 It lives in the ocean. It is flat. It has five legs.
What is it?

(A) An octopus
(B) A starfish
(C) A lizard

8 You go here to get money. You also save your money here. It is a place.
What is it?

(A) A bank
(B) A supermarket
(C) A post office

Lesson 5 47

Lesson 6　How does it look?

▶ **問題の形式**

このセクションでは，人や物の行動や特徴について，2つから3つの説明文が提示されます。それにあてはまる最も適切な語を選びましょう。
選択肢は3つあります。

ヒント
- 選択肢が動詞の場合には，問題文に代動詞doがあります。動詞を問題文に入れてみて，意味をなすかどうか考えましょう。
- あてはまらない語から，外していきましょう。

Example

Read and find the answer.
（問題を読んで，答えを選びましょう。）

1. You can do this at the beach. You can do it in a lake. You can also do it at a swimming pool.
   What are you doing?

   (A)　Sleeping
   (B)　Swimming
   (C)　Running

2. The skies are dark. You get wet if you go outside on this day. You need an umbrella.
   This day is _____.

   (A)　snowy
   (B)　rainy
   (C)　sunny

Answer

1. 答え　(B)

   これができるのは，海岸，湖，水泳プールです。したがって正解は (B) Swimming（泳いでいる）です。

2. 答え　(B)

   この天気だと，空は暗く，戸外ではぬれてしまいます。外に出るときには，傘を持っていく必要があります。したがって正解は (B) rainy（雨降り）です。

重要ポイント

形容詞 + 名詞

- A small and beautiful lake
- A kind teacher
- A soft cushion
- Yellow tigers

Be + 形容詞

- The lake is small and beautiful.
- The teacher is kind.
- The cushion is soft.
- The tigers are yellow.

確認問題

空欄をうめましょう。

1. They are happy girls.　　　　=　　The girls are _____.

2. It is _____ milk.　　=　　The milk is hot.

3. He is a tall teacher.　　　　=　　The teacher is _____.

Lesson 6

練習問題

Read and find the answer.
（問題を読んで，答えを選びましょう。）

1 When teachers ask questions, students are doing this.
When people call your name, you are doing it.
What are you doing?

- (A) Answering
- (B) Jumping
- (C) Shouting

NOTE
- ask questions
  ：質問する
- call one's name
  ：名前を呼ぶ

2 The rain does this. If glass does this, it breaks.
Trees _____ their leaves in fall.

- (A) pass
- (B) drop
- (C) slide

- glass: ガラス
- break: こわれる
- leaves: 葉
  （leafの複数形）
- fall: 秋

3 You have to do this first when you meet someone. People also do this when they start a presentation. If you don't do this, people don't know who you are.
What are you doing?

- (A) Introducing
- (B) Closing
- (C) Singing

- have to
  ：〜しなければならない
- presentation: 発表

4 People do this when they talk quietly. You must do this if you are in a library. Sometimes it is hard to hear when people do this.
What are they doing?

- (A) Lifting
- (B) Listening
- (C) Whispering

- quietly: 静かに
- library: 図書館
- hard: 難しい

5 People do this in the army. People also do this at a parade. A group of people walk together.
What are they doing?

  (A) Playing
  (B) Marching
  (C) Driving

· army: 軍隊
· parade: パレード

6 When you do this to something, it moves into the air. People do it in a baseball game. People do this and someone else catches.
What are they doing?

  (A) Hurting
  (B) Running
  (C) Throwing

· air: 空気
· baseball: 野球
· catch: 受け取る

7 If someone is in this condition, they are not healthy or do not have good muscles. They cannot move quickly or carry heavy things.
They are _____ .

  (A) strong
  (B) weak
  (C) smart

· condition: 状態
· muscle: 筋肉
· carry: 運ぶ
· heavy: 重い

8 You wear a hat and gloves to feel this way. The sun makes you feel this way, too. This has heat, but it is not enough to be hot.
What is it?

  (A) Hard
  (B) Warm
  (C) Cold

· wear: 着る
· hat: 帽子（ハット）
· gloves: 手袋
· heat: 熱
· enough to
 : 〜するのに十分な

Lesson 6   51

ミニテスト

Read and find the answer.

Fill in the correct circles on your answer sheet.

（問題を読んで，答えを選びましょう。解答欄の正しい丸をぬりつぶしましょう。）

	A	B	C
1.	Ⓐ	Ⓑ	Ⓒ
2.	Ⓐ	Ⓑ	Ⓒ
3.	Ⓐ	Ⓑ	Ⓒ
4.	Ⓐ	Ⓑ	Ⓒ

1 People don't like a room like this. You have to clean this room. It will make your mother angry.
This room is _____ .

- (A) tiny
- (B) dirty
- (C) huge

2 You do this after someone throws something to you. You do this with a baseball glove. You use your hands to stop and hold the object.
What are you doing?

- (A) Explaining
- (B) Catching
- (C) Crying

3 You do this and people follow. You do this if you tell people where to go. You also do this if you are the captain.
What are you doing?

- (A) Leading
- (B) Sending
- (C) Living

4 People do this with their bag. People have to do this with babies because they don't walk. People also do this to help their friends with something.
What are they doing?

- (A) Carrying
- (B) Touching
- (C) Giving

5.	Ⓐ	Ⓑ	Ⓒ
6.	Ⓐ	Ⓑ	Ⓒ
7.	Ⓐ	Ⓑ	Ⓒ
8.	Ⓐ	Ⓑ	Ⓒ

5 It is not rough or hard. If something is like this, it changes shape easily when you press it. Baby's skin is like this.
What is it?

   (A)   Soft
   (B)   Colorful
   (C)   Light

6 You do this to the candles on your birthday cake. You use your mouth. You have to take a deep breath to do it.
What are you doing?

   (A)   Screaming
   (B)   Singing
   (C)   Blowing

7 It is very fun. Sometimes you take an airplane, but not always. You go somewhere else to do this.
What are you doing?

   (A)   Flying
   (B)   Swinging
   (C)   Traveling

8 This person is nice. This person brings happiness to others. This person helps you.
This person is _____.

   (A)   ugly
   (B)   scary
   (C)   kind

Reading Part 3

Unit 4

Various Forms
(いろいろな文)

Lesson 7　When is the event?

Lesson 7: When is the event?

▶ **問題の形式**

このセクションでは，表，招待状，予定表，ポスターなど，いろいろな文章を読んで，それに続く質問に答えます。1つの問題文について，質問が4問あります。問題文はいろいろな形のものがあるので，このセクションはやや難しいかもしれません。

ヒント
- 実際の試験に出る文章の形式は多くありません。事前に，それぞれの形の文章を勉強しておきましょう。
- まず質問を読み，次に求められている情報を問題文から探します。
- 問題文が広告やポスターの場合，イベントの情報を注意して探しましょう。

Example

Read the invitation. Then answer questions 1 and 2.
（招待状を読んで，答えましょう。）

**Come to
my 9th birthday party!**

Friday, December 12th
5:00-8:00 p.m.

Pizza Land
1112 4th Street South
Los Angeles, California

Contact me, Steven 323-416-6656
supersteven@bob.com

---

1 What will they eat at the party?

(A) Sandwiches
(B) Pizza
(C) Hotdogs

2 When does the birthday party end?

(A) 5 PM
(B) 7 PM
(C) 8 PM

Answer

1. 答え （B）

この問題は，9歳の子の誕生パーティーに何が出るかです。パーティーはPizza Landでするのですから，パーティーではピザを食べるのだろうと考えられます。したがって正解は(B) Pizza（ピザ）です。

2. 答え （C）

この問題は，パーティーがいつ終わるのかを聞いています。招待状には，パーティーの時間が5p.m.から8p.m.と書かれています。したがって正解は(C)8PM（午後8時）です。

重要ポイント

日と日付

Thursday, January 1st, 2015

1) 月の初めの10日

1	2	3	4	5	6	7	8	9	10
first	second	third	fourth	fifth	sixth	seventh	eighth	ninth	tenth

2) 曜日の名前

| Monday (Mon.) | Tuesday (Tues.) | Wednesday (Wed.) | Thursday (Thurs.) | Friday (Fri.) | Saturday (Sat.) | Sunday (Sun.) |

3) 月の名前

January (Jan.)	February (Feb.)	March (Mar.)	April (Apr.)
May (May)	June (Jun.)	July (Jul.)	August (Aug.)
September (Sept.)	October (Oct.)	November (Nov.)	December (Dec.)

確認問題

英語で日付を書きましょう。

1. 1998年3月19日火曜日　→　_____

2. 2008年11月25日土曜日　→　_____

練習問題

Read about Tony. Then answer questions 1 to 3.
（トニーについてのメモを読んで，答えましょう。）

Tony's Yearbook
Read about Tony!

Likes movies about	Hobbies
· Space · Adventure · Animals	· Baseball · Reading books · Playing with friends

Favorite Subjects	Favorite Books
· Math · Science · Gym	· Harry Potter · The Giving Tree · The Little Prince

1 What movie would Tony like?

  (A) A wild animal story
  (B) A prince and princess story
  (C) A comic story

2 Which subject does Tony like?

  (A) English
  (B) Math
  (C) Art

3 What does Tony like to do in his free time?

  (A) Play with a brother
  (B) Play soccer
  (C) Read books

NOTE

· movie: 映画
· space: 宇宙
· adventure: 冒険
· hobby: 趣味
· favorite: 好きな
　（気に入っている）
· subject: 科目
· gym: 体育

Read the menu. Then answer questions 4 to 6.
（メニューを読んで，答えましょう。）

Jefferson Elementary School
Lunch Menu

Please choose from the menu!

Main Course	Vegetable	Fruit	Drink
Spaghetti	Carrot	Apple	Apple Juice
Rice and Beans	Salad	Orange	Orange Juice
Fried Rice	Celery	Banana	Iced Water
Beef Soup	Cherry Tomato	Kiwi	Milk

NOTE

- main course：メインの料理
- drink: 飲み物
- spaghetti：スパゲッティ
- bean: 豆
- fried rice: チャーハン
- celery: セロリ
- beef: 牛肉

4 Why does the school have this menu?

(A) For lunch time
(B) For snack time
(C) For dinner time

5 What vegetable can the students eat?

(A) Onion
(B) Carrot
(C) Broccoli

6 Which drink is not in the menu?

(A) Orange Juice
(B) Milk
(C) Iced Tea

ミニテスト

Read Elizabeth's plan. Then answer questions 1 to 4.
Fill in the correct circles on your answer sheet.
（日課表を読んで，答えましょう。解答欄の正しい丸をぬりつぶしましょう。）

My Daily Planner
Elizabeth Turner

8:30-8:45	Arrive at school
9:00-10:00	Math Class - Homework
10:00-11:00	Gym Class
11:00-12:00	Science Class
12:00-12:30	Lunch
12:45-1:00	Recess
1:00-1:30	Music Class
1:45-2:45	English Class
2:45-3:00	Take the bus home!

1.	Ⓐ	Ⓑ	Ⓒ
2.	Ⓐ	Ⓑ	Ⓒ
3.	Ⓐ	Ⓑ	Ⓒ
4.	Ⓐ	Ⓑ	Ⓒ

1 Who wrote the schedule?

    (A)   A parent

    (B)   A student

    (C)   A teacher

2 For what class does the student have homework?

    (A)   Math

    (B)   Science

    (C)   English

3 Which is the shortest activity?

    (A)   Lunch

    (B)   Science

    (C)   Recess

4 How does the student get home from school?

    (A)   By foot

    (B)   By bus

    (C)   By car

Read the handout. Then answer questions 5 to 8.
Fill in the correct circles on your answer sheet.
(チラシを読んで，答えましょう。解答欄の正しい丸をぬりつぶしましょう。)

Sports Day!

Longfellow Elementary School
Invites you to our yearly event!

Events include:

Relay Race

Jump Rope Contest

There will be two teams.
Every student participates. Come and see your children run!

Friday, April 17th
1:00-4:00 PM
At Longfellow Elementary Field

5.	Ⓐ	Ⓑ	Ⓒ
6.	Ⓐ	Ⓑ	Ⓒ
7.	Ⓐ	Ⓑ	Ⓒ
8.	Ⓐ	Ⓑ	Ⓒ

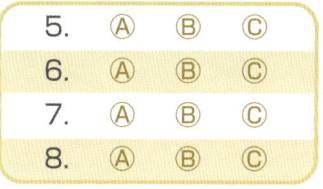

5 How many teams will there be?

(A) Two

(B) Three

(C) Four

6 Who will participate in the event?

(A) Students on sports teams

(B) Parents and students

(C) All students

7 Where will the event be?

(A) Longfellow cafeteria

(B) Longfellow field

(C) Longfellow classroom

8 Which activity will the students NOT do?

(A) Relay Race

(B) Soccer

(C) Jump Rope

Reading Part 3

Unit 5

Short Passages
(短い文章)

》Lesson 8　What is the letter about?

Lesson 8: What is the letter about?

▶ **問題の形式**

このセクションでは，短い文章を読んでそれに続く質問に答えます。本書では，手紙，Eメール，説明文や物語など，いろいろな短い文章を載せています。これを読んで，読解力をつけましょう。

(Lexile: 400L~600L)

ヒント
- 手紙とEメールの場合は，送り手と受け手がだれかを考えましょう。受け手の名前は文章の初めに，送り手の名前は最後に書いてあります。
- 手紙の目的を考えて，その部分に注目するとよいでしょう。
- 内容について，いくつかの質問があります。最初に質問を読んで，その後で文章を読むほうが，答えを見つけやすくなります。

Example

Read the email. Then answer questions 1 and 2.
（Eメールを読んで，質問に答えましょう。）

Gloria,

I made a mistake! I forgot to write down when the math test is. This unit was so difficult for me. I need to know when the test is. Could you send me an email back about when it is? Also, do you want to study for the test together? We could do it at my house. My mom will make us some snacks!

Your friend,
Katie

1 Who made the mistake?

(A) Gloria
(B) Katie
(C) The mom

2 What was the mistake?

(A) Someone didn't study.
(B) Someone forgot to go to math class.
(C) Someone forgot when a test is.

Answer

1. 答え　(B)

Eメールを送ったのはケイティで，最初に「私が間違いをしました」と書いています。したがって正解は(B) Katieです。

2. 答え　(C)

このEメールは，数学の試験の予定についてです。ケイティは，書きとめておくのを忘れたため，試験がいつなのかを聞いています。したがって正解は(C) Someone forgot when a test is.（試験がいつなのか忘れた）です。

重要ポイント

疑問文を作る

Who	ex) Who is your brother?
What	ex) What is that?
When	ex) When did he come back?
Where	ex) Where do you live?
Why	ex) Why does she go there?
How	ex) How are you today?
	ex) How many pencils do you have?

確認問題

空欄を，Wh-の語のどれか，もしくはHowでうめましょう。

1. _____ did she go yesterday?　　She went to **the museum**.
2. _____ drew this picture?　　**Sarah** drew it.
3. _____ is your favorite food?　　My favorite food is **pizza**.
4. _____ were you sad?　　I **lost my book**.
5. _____ is your new room?　　It is **small but nice**.
6. _____ do you go to bed?　　I go to bed **at 10 o'clock**.

Lesson 8

練習問題

Read the letter. Then answer questions 1 and 2.

（手紙を読んで，質問に答えましょう。）

Dear Grandma,

My dad tells me that you are very sick. I hope you get better soon. I can't wait to visit you again. I want to play the card game we played last time! We won't be able to play if you are still sick. I drink lots of water when I am sick. I think it helps me get better! You should drink lots of water and get some rest. I will see you soon.

Your Grandson,
Tom

（80語）

NOTE

- visit: 訪問する
- again: もう一度
- still: 今でもまだ

- get better:（具合が）よくなる
- can't wait to: 待ちきれない（早く〜したい）
- be able to:〜することができる
- get rest: 休息する（体を休める）

1 What does Tom do when he is sick?

(A) Write a letter
(B) Play a game
(C) Drink lots of water

2 Who is Tom writing the letter to?

(A) His dad
(B) His grandson
(C) His grandma

Read the text. Then answer questions 3 and 4.

(文章を読んで，質問に答えましょう。)

> There are many useful tools in the world. One of them is the boomerang. A boomerang is an object that you throw into the air. It then returns to your hand! Long ago, people used boomerangs for hunting and even starting a fire. They are very strong. These days, they are used for fun! You can go to the store and buy a boomerang.
>
> (64語)

NOTE

- tool: 道具
- boomerang
  : ブーメラン
- object: 物体
- throw: 投げる
- air: 空中
- return: 返ってくる
- hunt: 狩りをする

- long ago
  : ずっと昔に
- start a fire
  : 火をおこす

3 When did people use boomerangs before?

(A) When they hunted
(B) When they played
(C) When they went to the store

4 What does the boomerang do?

(A) It flies really far and falls to the ground.
(B) It flies in the air and returns.
(C) It is a target for birds.

ミニテスト

Read the letter. Then answer questions 1 and 2.
Fill in the correct circles on your answer sheet.
（手紙を読んで質問に答えましょう。解答欄の正しい丸をぬりつぶしましょう。）

1. Ⓐ Ⓑ Ⓒ
2. Ⓐ Ⓑ Ⓒ

Dear Uncle John,

I want to tell you how much fun I had at the zoo. This vacation was really fun for me. I really enjoyed seeing the lions and tigers. Oh, and I cannot forget about the penguins! I liked watching the penguins swim most of all. I hope all my trips can be as fun as this. And I cannot wait to see you again! Thank you so much for bringing me to the zoo.

Sincerely,
Andrew

（79語）

1 Why is Andrew writing to his Uncle John?

(A) To thank his uncle for taking him to the zoo
(B) To see if his uncle wants to go to the zoo
(C) To give his uncle a birthday message

2 What did Andrew like most?

(A) The lions
(B) The tigers
(C) The penguins

Read the story. Then answer questions 3 and 4. Fill in the correct circles on your answer sheet.

3. Ⓐ Ⓑ Ⓒ
4. Ⓐ Ⓑ Ⓒ

（文章を読んで質問に答えましょう。解答欄の正しい丸をぬりつぶしましょう。）

My favorite toy is a skateboard. I got it for my birthday when I turned eleven years old. I ride it during the summertime. I really like to ride it in the park. I can do nice tricks on my skateboard. I can jump off my board or spin in a circle! My skateboard is blue with red stripes. Both of them are my favorite colors. I can ride it with my friends also. It is a lot of fun.

（80語）

3 What is NOT a trick the child can do?

(A) Jump off the board
(B) Spin in a circle
(C) Jump over a car

4 Where does the child like to go with the skateboard?

(A) A friend's house
(B) The park
(C) The sidewalk

Listening
Part 1

Unit 6
Picture Descriptions
(絵を見て聞いて答えよう〈状態〉)

Lesson 9 What is on the desk?

Lesson 9   What is on the desk?

▶ **問題の形式**

このセクションでは，英語の指示を聞き，それにしたがって3つの絵の中から絵を選びましょう。聞き取りが始まるまでに，絵を見て考えておくと，答えを選びやすくなります。

ヒント
- 聞き取りが始まる前に，それぞれの絵の特徴を見つけておきましょう。
- 人や動物の場合は，何をやっているかなどを注意して聞き取りましょう。
- 物の場合は，形，大きさ，色，数などのポイントをしっかり聞き取りましょう。

Example

Listen to the sentence. Look at the pictures. Choose the correct picture.
（文章を聞いて，正しい絵を選びましょう。）

1. (A) 　(B) 　(C)

Script　She is drinking water.

2. (A) 　(B) 　(C)

Script　There is a doll under the bench.

Answer

1. 答え **(B)**

   この問題では，この人が何をしているのかを答えます。水を飲んでいる女の子の絵を探しましょう。正解は (B) です。

2. 答え **(A)**

   この問題では，絵にかいてある物の位置を答えます。ベンチの下に人形がある絵を探しましょう。正解は (A) です。

重要ポイント

- **instead of**　〜ではなく，〜の代わりに

  He is watching TV **instead of** a movie.
  They take a taxi **instead of** a bus.

  やってみよう！

  She is eating _____ _____ **instead of** _____
  _____ .

  彼女は，バナナではなくリンゴを食べているところです。

- **too ... to ~**　あまりにも…なので〜できない

  I'm **too** tired **to** do my homework.
  He is **too** busy **to** go for a walk.

  やってみよう！

  Science is **too** _____ **to** _____ .

  理科は，あまりにも難しいので勉強できません（理科は，勉強するにはあまりにも難解です）。

Lesson 9

練習問題

Listen to the sentence. Look at the pictures. Choose the correct picture.

（文章を聞いて，正しい絵を選びましょう。）

1

(A)　(B)　(C)

NOTE

・around: 〜のまわりに
・neck: 首

2

(A) 　(B) 　(C)

・hold: 〜を持って（抱えて）いる
・present: プレゼント

3

(A) 　(B) 　(C)

・couple: 2人の人，カップル
・walk:（動物を）散歩させる

4

(A) 　(B) 　(C)

・in the middle of: 〜の真ん中に
・pond: 池

5
(A) (B) (C)

6
(A) (B) (C)

7
(A) (B) (C)

8
(A) (B) (C)

NOTE

・road: 道路
・empty: すいている，空の

・a pair of: 一組のメガネのレンズは2枚あるので，メガネは a pair of glasses と言います。a pair を省略して glasses と言うこともできます。
他の例）a pair of socks, a pair of scissors

・both: 両方（2つあるものについて）
・the same: 同じ

・sat: sit（座る）の過去形
・next to: 〜の次に，〜のとなりに，〜の横に
・instead of: 〜ではなく（〜の代わりに）

Lesson 9　77

ミニテスト

**Listen to the sentence. Look at the pictures.
Fill in the correct circles on your answer sheet.**
(文章を聞いて，解答欄の正しい丸をぬりつぶしましょう。)

1.	Ⓐ	Ⓑ	Ⓒ
2.	Ⓐ	Ⓑ	Ⓒ
3.	Ⓐ	Ⓑ	Ⓒ
4.	Ⓐ	Ⓑ	Ⓒ

1
(A) 　　(B) 　　(C) 

2
(A) 　　(B) 　　(C) 

3
(A) 　　(B) 　　(C) 

4
(A) 　　(B) 　　(C) 

78　Unit 6

5.	Ⓐ	Ⓑ	Ⓒ
6.	Ⓐ	Ⓑ	Ⓒ
7.	Ⓐ	Ⓑ	Ⓒ
8.	Ⓐ	Ⓑ	Ⓒ

5

(A)   (B)   (C)

6

(A)   (B)   (C)

7

(A)   (B)   (C)

8

(A)   (B)   (C)

書き取り

ミニテスト

Listen to *Mini Test* again. Write the correct word in each blank.
（ミニテストをもう一度聞き，_____にあてはまる単語を書きましょう。）

1 There [1]a _____ three [2]c _____ on a cake.

2 The man is [3]p _____ his cat.

3 She is too [4]s _____ f _____ the sweater.

4 She [5]t _____ o _____ the television.

5 The boy [6]h _____ his knee.

6 He [7]w _____ first [8]p _____ in the singing contest.

7 The little girl is too [9]s _____ to [10]s _____ the snake.

8 The blue cup is [11]s _____ than the yellow cup, but is [12]b _____ than the red cup.

80 Unit 6

Memo

Listening Part 2

Unit 7

Instructions
（絵を見て聞いて答えよう〈指示〉）

> Lesson 10   What did she say?

Lesson 10 What did she say?

▶ **問題の形式**

このセクションでは，絵の内容に関する短い説明や指示を聞き，それを表す正しい絵を3つの絵の中から選んで答えます。

ヒント
- 3つの絵はどこが違うのか，すばやく見つけましょう。
- よく気をつけて，指示の内容を聞き取りましょう。
- 「するべきこと」と「してはいけないこと」をはっきり区別しましょう。

Example

Listen to the sentences. Look at the pictures. Choose the correct picture.
（文章を聞いて，正しい絵を選びましょう。）

1

(A) 　(B) 　(C)

Script
T: Good morning, everyone. Please hang your backpack on a hook by the door.

2

(A) 　(B) 　(C)

Script
M: It is raining outside. Please put on your rain boots and take an umbrella, so you don't get dirty or wet.

84　Unit 7

Answer

1. 答え　(A)

   ドア近くのフックに背負ってきたランドセルを生徒たちが掛けている絵を探しましょう。正解は (A) です。

2. 答え　(C)

   長靴をはいて傘をさしている人の絵を探しましょう。正解は (C) です。

重要ポイント

- **I'd like to ~**　私は~したいと思う

  I'd like to have a new phone.
  I'd like to sit next to Sally.

  やってみよう！
  I'd like to _____ _____ _____.
  私は自転車に乗りたいと思います。

- **It's time to ~**　~をする時間だ

  It's time to finish the class.
  It's time to go to bed.

  やってみよう！
  It's time to _____ _____.
  さようならを言う時間です。

練習問題

Listen to the sentences. Look at the pictures. Choose the correct picture.

(文章を聞いて，正しい絵を選びましょう。)

1
(A)   (B)   (C)

2
(A)   (B)   (C)

3
(A)   (B)   (C)

4
(A)   (B)   (C)

NOTE

- partner:（ダンス，ゲーム，仕事などをいっしょにする）相手
- two times: 2回（2度）

- yell: 大きな声でどなる
- hurt: 傷める（けがをさせる）

- turn off:（電気を）消す，（ガス・水などを）止める
- save: 節約する
  save energy: エネルギーを節約する
  save time: 時間を節約する

- share: 他の人といっしょに使う
- one of you: あなたがたのうちの1人

86   Unit 7

5

(A)   (B)   (C)

- messy: よごれた
- paint: 絵の具, 絵の具をぬる

6

(A)   (B)   (C)

- give back: 〜を返す
- took: take（取る）の過去形
- without asking: 聞きもせずに, 断りなく

7

(A)   (B)   (C)

- would like to 〜: 〜したいと思う
- introduce: 紹介する
- move to: 〜へ引っ越す

8

(A)   (B)   (C)

- like: 〜のような
  healthy foods like fruits
  : 果物のような健康によい食べ物
- test results: 検査結果
- too much sugar: 多すぎる糖分
- plan a diet: ダイエットを計画する

Lesson 10

ミニテスト

CD1 6 Listen to the sentences. Look at the pictures.
Fill in the correct circles on your answer sheet.
（文章を聞いて，解答欄の正しい丸をぬりつぶしましょう。）

1.	Ⓐ	Ⓑ	Ⓒ
2.	Ⓐ	Ⓑ	Ⓒ
3.	Ⓐ	Ⓑ	Ⓒ
4.	Ⓐ	Ⓑ	Ⓒ

1
(A)    (B)    (C) 

2
(A)    (B)    (C) 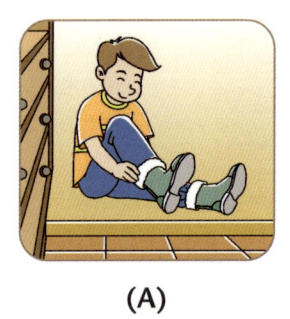

3
(A)    (B)    (C) 

4
(A)    (B)    (C) 

88　Unit 7

5.	Ⓐ	Ⓑ	Ⓒ
6.	Ⓐ	Ⓑ	Ⓒ
7.	Ⓐ	Ⓑ	Ⓒ
8.	Ⓐ	Ⓑ	Ⓒ

5

(A)　　　(B)　　　(C)

6

(A)　　　(B)　　　(C)

7

(A)　　　(B)　　　(C)

8

(A)　　　(B)　　　(C)

Lesson 10

書き取り

ミニテスト

Listen to *Mini Test* again. Write the correct word in each blank.
（ミニテストをもう一度聞き，＿＿＿にあてはまる単語を書きましょう。）

1. W: Now it's time to ¹f_____ t_____ t_____. Raise your hand if you're finished writing all your answers.

2. W: We are going to go for a long walk. Please ²p_____ _____ your running shoes that are sitting by the door.

3. M: I am getting very old. Sometimes I need help. Can you please ³c_____ o_____ here and help me out of my chair? Just ⁴t_____ _____ h_____ while I try to stand up.

4. M: Today, we will ⁵l_____ a_____ wild animals. Please sit with your hands in your lap and watch this video. It will not ⁶t_____ a very long t_____.

5 W: Sam, your teeth look very yellow. You should try ⁷b_____ y_____ t_____ with this toothpaste. Here is a new toothbrush too.

6 W: Stop running in the hallway! You need to calm down and walk slowly. If you are running too fast, you might accidently ⁸b_____ i_____ another student or teacher.

7 M: To help you memorize your vocabulary words, we're going to make flashcards. Please write the ⁹w_____ on the front of the card and write the ¹⁰m_____ of the word on the back of the card. These flashcards will help you during your quiz.

8 M: Hey, I can see the spaghetti noodles in your mouth. Please ¹¹c_____ y_____ f_____ with your mouth closed. If your mouth ¹²_____ o_____ while you eat, everyone can see the chewed food, and it is very noisy.

Listening Part 3

Unit 8

Short Conversations
(短い会話)

› Lesson 11   Can you help me?

› Lesson 12   How are you feeling?

Lesson 11 Can you help me?

▶ 問題の形式

このセクションでは，学校生活について2人の短い会話を聞きます。
質問に対する正しい答えを選びましょう。
選択肢は3つあります。

> **ヒント**
> - 学校や図書館，病院，スクールバスの中でよく聞くような簡単な会話が流れます。
> - 話している人の言うことを理解して，一番よく合う答えを見つけましょう。
> - 問題用紙には選択肢が書かれていません。質問と3つの選択肢をしっかりと聞き取りましょう。

Example

CD1 7 Listen to the conversations. Which conversation sounds correct?
（会話を聞き，正しい会話を選びましょう。）

1　(A)　　　(B)　　　(C)

Script
B: Do you want to play on the slide?
(A) Yes, of course.
(B) No, she is not nice.
(C) Yes, we better go home.

2　(A)　　　(B)　　　(C)

Script
B: The slide is really fun. What do you want to do next?
(A) Yes, it's right here.
(B) Let's go on the swings.
(C) Sure, that would be fine.

Answer

1. 答え **(A)**

   「滑り台で遊びたいですか」という質問に対する答は，(A) Yes, of course.（はい，もちろんです）です。

2. 答え **(B)**

   「滑り台は本当に楽しいですね。次は，何をしたいですか」という質問に対する答えは，(B) Let's go on the swings.（ぶらんこをしよう）です。

重要ポイント

- **be good at ~**　〜が得意だ，〜が上手だ

  Eric **is good at** math.

  I**'m good at** playing the piano.

  やってみよう！

  My father **is good at** ＿＿＿＿＿＿＿ .

  父は運転が上手です。

- **Do you think ~?**　あなたは〜と思いますか。

  Do you think she is smart?

  Do you think you are a good son?

  やってみよう！

  Do you think ＿＿＿＿＿ ＿＿＿＿＿ ＿＿＿＿＿ ＿＿＿＿＿ ?

  あなたは彼が先生だと思いますか。

練習問題

Listen to the conversations. Which conversation sounds correct?
（会話を聞いて，正しい会話を選びましょう。）

1
    (A)   (B)   (C)

2
    (A)   (B)   (C)

3
    (A)   (B)   (C)

4
    (A)   (B)   (C)

NOTE

試験用紙には，答えの選択肢を載せていません。会話を聞きながら直接意味をとり，間違っている選択肢を消していきましょう。

- by the door: ドアの横に
  byは〜の横，〜のわきを表します。
  by the river: 川辺で
- soon: もうすぐ
- be good at 〜 : 〜が上手だ

- practice: 練習
  swim practice: 水泳の練習
  piano practice: ピアノの練習
- swam: swim（泳ぐ）の過去形
- swimming pool: プール
- win the race: 競技・競争に勝つ
- try my best: 最善を尽くす

5
(A)　　　(B)　　　(C)

6
(A)　　　(B)　　　(C)

7
(A)　　　(B)　　　(C)

8
(A)　　　(B)　　　(C)

NOTE

- scratch: すりむく
- bandage: 包帯
- trip on the stairs: 階段でつまずく

- wrap up your knee: ひざに包帯を巻く
- interesting: 面白い、興味深い
- do my best: 最善を尽くす

- what kind of ~: どのような（種類の）〜
- adventure: 冒険
- scare: 怖がらせる

- library card: 図書貸し出しカード
- over there: あちら（のほう）に

Lesson 11　97

ミニテスト

Listen to the conversations. Which conversation sounds correct? Fill in the correct circles on your answer sheet.
（会話を聞いて，解答欄の正しい丸をぬりつぶしましょう。）

1. Ⓐ Ⓑ Ⓒ
2. Ⓐ Ⓑ Ⓒ
3. Ⓐ Ⓑ Ⓒ
4. Ⓐ Ⓑ Ⓒ

1
(A)　　　(B)　　　(C)

2
(A)　　　(B)　　　(C)

3
(A)　　　(B)　　　(C)

4
(A)　　　(B)　　　(C)

	Ⓐ	Ⓑ	Ⓒ
5.	Ⓐ	Ⓑ	Ⓒ
6.	Ⓐ	Ⓑ	Ⓒ
7.	Ⓐ	Ⓑ	Ⓒ
8.	Ⓐ	Ⓑ	Ⓒ

5

(A)　　　(B)　　　(C)

6

(A)　　　(B)　　　(C)

7

(A)　　　(B)　　　(C)

8

(A)　　　(B)　　　(C)

書き取り

ミニテスト

Listen to *Mini Test* again. Write the correct word in each blank.
(ミニテストをもう一度聞き，_____にあてはまる単語を書きましょう。)

1   G: Which one is your locker?

   (A)   I am right-handed.
   (B)   The one ¹_____ t_____ l_____ .
   (C)   Please walk forward.

2   G: Can you ²h_____ _____ c_____ my books to class?

   (A)   Sure, I can help you.
   (B)   Yes, I have many books.
   (C)   The history book ³_____ h_____ .

3   M: Where do you live?

   (A)   Please stop the bus.
   (B)   Just ⁴d_____ t_____ s_____ .
   (C)   You are a good driver.

4   M: Please find a seat and sit down.

   (A)   I can't see anything.
   (B)   It's very cold ⁵_____ h_____ .
   (C)   But all the seats ⁶a_____ f_____ .

5 W: Please [7] s_____ d_____ at this table to read.

(A) I like my reading teacher.

(B) Thank you, I will.

(C) I can't decide.

6 W: Is this book [8] h_____ _____ r_____?

(A) No, I can't look right now.

(B) Maybe, it's hard to [9] c_____ just one.

(C) Yes, the book is very hard to understand.

7 M: [10] H_____ m_____ do you know about math?

(A) I think there are too many.

(B) I don't really [11] k_____ _____ l_____.

(C) That sounds fun.

8 M: Can you answer this math problem?

(A) Sure, [12] _____ c_____ t_____.

(B) I read it last week.

(C) I said many things.

Lesson 12 — How are you feeling?

▶ **問題の形式**

このセクションでは，2人の日常会話を聞きます。
質問に対する正しい答えを選びましょう。
選択肢は3つあります。

ヒント
- お店やペットショップ，レストランなどでよく聞くような簡単な会話が流れます。
- 会話の正しい意味を理解して，一番よく合う答えを見つけましょう。
- 問題用紙には選択肢が書かれていません。質問と3つの選択肢をしっかりと聞き取りましょう。

Example

CD1-10 Listen to the conversations. Which conversation sounds correct?
（会話を聞いて，正しい会話を選びましょう。）

1   (A)   (B)   (C)

Script
W: Welcome to Super Shoes. What size shoe do you wear?
(A) I can't see them.
(B) I wear a size seven.
(C) Those tennis shoes look nice.

2   (A)   (B)   (C)

Script
W: The shoes come in many different colors. Which color would you like?
(A) The hat is green.
(B) I will take the blue pair.
(C) My mother likes the yellow color.

Answer

1. 答え (B)

「どのサイズの靴をおはきですか」という質問に対する答えは，(B) I wear a size seven.（サイズ7をはきます）です。

2. 答え (B)

「何色がお好きですか」という質問に対する答えは，(B) I will take the blue pair.（青いのをください）です。

重要ポイント

- **Would you like to ~?**　〜をなさいますか，〜をしてみたいですか

    Would you like to come to my house?
    Would you like to leave a message?

    やってみよう！
    Would you like to _____ _____ _____ _____ ?
    私たちといっしょに，キャンプに行きますか。

- **look like ~**　〜に似ている

    You **look like** an actor.
    It **looks like** a new school bus.

    やってみよう！
    He **looks like** _____ _____ .
    彼は彼のお父さんに似ている。

練習問題

Listen to the conversations. Which conversation sounds correct?
（会話を聞いて，正しい会話を選びましょう。）

NOTE

試験用紙には，答えの選択肢を載せていません。会話を聞きながら直接意味をとり，間違いの選択肢を消していきましょう。

1
    (A)   (B)   (C)

- headache: 頭痛
  have a headache: 頭が痛い

2
    (A)   (B)   (C)

- bump: ぶつける
- corner: 角
- lie down: 寝る（横になる）
- feel dizzy: めまいがする

3
    (A)   (B)   (C)

- trip and fall: 踏み外して転ぶ
- watch your step: 足元に気をつける

4
    (A)   (B)   (C)

- scan your bus card: バスカードをスキャンする
- scan: スキャン（読み取り）する
- good to see you: お会いできてうれしい

5
      (A)   (B)   (C)

NOTE
- which: どちらの（どっちの）
- fur: 毛
- fluffy: ふわふわしている

6
      (A)   (B)   (C)

- right now: 今すぐに

7
      (A)   (B)   (C)

- favorite: 大好きなもの（気に入っているもの）

8
      (A)   (B)   (C)

- try on: 着てみる（試着する）
- another: 別の（他の）
- a little: 少し

Lesson 12

ミニテスト

Listen to the conversations. Which conversation sounds correct? Fill in the correct circles on your answer sheet.
（会話を聞いて，解答欄の正しい丸をぬりつぶしましょう。）

1. Ⓐ Ⓑ Ⓒ
2. Ⓐ Ⓑ Ⓒ
3. Ⓐ Ⓑ Ⓒ
4. Ⓐ Ⓑ Ⓒ

1

(A)　　　　　(B)　　　　　(C)

2

(A)　　　　　(B)　　　　　(C)

3

(A)　　　　　(B)　　　　　(C)

4

(A)　　　　　(B)　　　　　(C)

5.	Ⓐ	Ⓑ	Ⓒ
6.	Ⓐ	Ⓑ	Ⓒ
7.	Ⓐ	Ⓑ	Ⓒ
8.	Ⓐ	Ⓑ	Ⓒ

5

(A) (B) (C)

6

(A) (B) (C)

7

(A) (B) (C)

8

(A) (B) (C)

書き取り

ミニテスト

Listen to *Mini Test* again. Write the correct word in each blank.
(ミニテストをもう一度聞き，＿＿＿にあてはまる単語を書きましょう。)

1. **M:** Hello there, ¹h_____ c_____ _____ help you?

   (A) Yes, it's on the table.

   (B) Hi, my cat is very sick.

   (C) Now I feel happy.

2. **M:** I think your cat will ²f_____ f_____ in a few days.

   (A) I feel very sad today.

   (B) You are ³v_____ k_____ _____ _____.

   (C) Thank you, I was worried.

3. **W:** Hey, I ⁴h_____ _____ j_____ for you.

   (A) I can't remember.

   (B) Oh really? What is it?

   (C) Do you like your job?

4. **W:** Can you please ⁵w_____ t_____ f_____ for me?

   (A) OK, I won't.

   (B) Yes, I certainly will.

   (C) You can ⁶c_____ _____ s_____ _____.

5 W: Would you like ⁷s_____ i_____ c_____ for dessert?

 (A) Sure, that sounds good.

 (B) I cannot go there.

 (C) No, I don't like you.

6 W: What flavor of ice cream do you want?

 (A) ⁸J_____ t_____ p_____ .

 (B) ⁹P_____ _____ the sugar.

 (C) I will have chocolate.

7 W: Welcome to Dazzling Dresses. There is a ¹⁰b_____ s_____ _____ dresses today.

 (A) Great, I love sales.

 (B) There is a 50% discount.

 (C) I heard him ¹¹_____ t_____ r_____ .

8 W: It ¹²l_____ l_____ you found the perfect dress.

 (A) I can't find the zipper.

 (B) No, his pants are too big.

 (C) I agree. This dress is very lovely.

Lesson 12   109

Listening Part 4

Unit 9

Long Conversations
(長い会話)

› Lesson 13   What does he want?
› Lesson 14   What will she do next?

Lesson 13 What does he want?

▶ 問題の形式

このセクションでは，2人が学校で行う会話を聞き取ります。
最も正しい答えを選びましょう。選択肢は3つあります。

> **ヒント**
> ・生徒と先生，図書館員と生徒，2人の友達などが学校で行う会話が流れます。
> ・会話が流れる前に，質問文と答えにさっと目を通しておきましょう。それから会話を聞き取り，関連する情報を探しましょう。
> ・聞き取りながら，間違っていると思う選択肢があれば，外していきましょう。

Example

CD1 13 Listen to a conversation and answer a question.
（会話を聞いて，問題に答えましょう。）

1 What does the boy want?

(A) An eraser
(B) Some paper
(C) One more pencil

2 What will the boy do next?

(A) Read a book
(B) Hang up his coat
(C) Sit down in a chair

Script

1. B1: This test looks hard.
   B2: I agree. Do you have a pencil I can borrow?
   B1: Yeah, here you go.
   B2: Thanks, I just want to have an extra one.

2. W: Hello. Welcome to my classroom.
   B: Thanks. I am excited to start a new class.
   W: How about you find somewhere to sit?
   B: OK, I'll do that right now.

Answer

1. 答え　(C)

これは試験中にした2人の少年の会話です。1人が，予備の鉛筆を別の少年から1本借りたいと言っています。したがって，「少年は何がほしいですか」という質問に対する答えは，(C) One more pencil.（鉛筆をもう1本）です。

2. 答え　(C)

これは先生と少年の会話です。先生は少年に，席を見つけて座るよう言い，少年は「はい，すぐそうします」と言いました。したがって，少年が次に行う行動は，(C) Sit down in a char.（いすに座る）です。

重要ポイント

- **Why don't you ~?**　〜したらどうですか，〜しませんか

    Why don't you play outside?
    Why don't you use the library at school?

    やってみよう！
    Why don't you ＿＿＿＿＿ ＿＿＿＿＿ ＿＿＿＿＿, Alice?
    あなたの友人のAliceに電話をしたらどうですか。

- **That's why ~**　それが〜の理由だ，それだから〜だ

    That's why I was late for school.
    That's why she has so many friends.

    やってみよう！
    That's why I ＿＿＿＿＿ ＿＿＿＿＿ ＿＿＿＿＿ ＿＿＿＿＿.
    それが，宿題をしなかった理由です（だから，私は宿題をしませんでした）。

Lesson 13　113

練習問題

Listen to a conversation and answer a question.
（会話を聞いて，問題に答えましょう。）

1 What will the girl do next?

- (A) Fix a hook in the closet
- (B) Put her jacket in the closet
- (C) Hang her backpack by the door

NOTE
- hang up: 掛ける（つるす）
- hook:（洋服を掛ける）フック
- closet: クローゼット
- fix: 固定する，留める

2 What will the boy do next?

- (A) Sit down at a table
- (B) Find a book about bears
- (C) Finish his research project

- research: 研究（調査）
- a bunch of: たくさんの
- look at ~: ～を見る

3 Why does the girl need a name tag?

- (A) It is for her homework.
- (B) It is the last day of school.
- (C) So her classmates know her name.

- the first day of school: 初めての登校日
- name tag: 名札
- that's why ~: それが～の理由だ

4 What will the girls do next?

- (A) Read more action books
- (B) Go home to eat pizza
- (C) Go to the cafeteria

- full of ~: ～でいっぱいの（～がたくさんある）
- kind of hungry: ちょっとおなかが空いた

5 What will the boy do next?

(A) Bring a new paint brush
(B) Clean his paint brushes
(C) Paint his partner's face

6 Why does the girl not want to sing?

(A) She is nervous about singing.
(B) Her teacher doesn't like her.
(C) She is better at painting.

7 What will the girl do next?

(A) Look at the calendar
(B) Plan the next field trip
(C) Ask the teacher a question

8 What does the boy want to do?

(A) Write about his art teacher
(B) Write about his math teacher
(C) Write about the science experiment

NOTE

- look exactly like ~
  : ～にそっくり（同じ）に見える
- Good job!: よくできました。
- be covered in ~
  : ～だらけだ
- sink: 流し

- nervous: 不安な，怖い
- one time: （以前）ある時に
- laugh at ~: ～を笑う
- make mistakes: 間違える（ミスをする）

- field trip: 遠足
- why don't you ~?
  : ～したらどうですか
- plan: 計画を立てる

- journal: 日記
- science experiment
  : 理科の実験
- what I enjoy the most
  : 私が一番楽しいもの

ミニテスト

Listen to a conversation and answer a question. Fill in the correct circles on your answer sheet.
（会話を聞いて，解答欄の正しい丸をぬりつぶしましょう。）

1.	Ⓐ	Ⓑ	Ⓒ
2.	Ⓐ	Ⓑ	Ⓒ
3.	Ⓐ	Ⓑ	Ⓒ
4.	Ⓐ	Ⓑ	Ⓒ

1 What does the girl want to do?

- (A) Paint in art class
- (B) Draw a pretty cup
- (C) Make a clay bowl

2 What will the boy do next?

- (A) Tie his shoelaces
- (B) Change his shoes
- (C) Run around the track

3 Where will the girl go next?

- (A) To the bathroom
- (B) To the video room
- (C) To the movie theater

4 What do the girls agree to do?

- (A) Play a review game
- (B) Sit by each other in class
- (C) Study for the test together

5.	Ⓐ	Ⓑ	Ⓒ
6.	Ⓐ	Ⓑ	Ⓒ
7.	Ⓐ	Ⓑ	Ⓒ
8.	Ⓐ	Ⓑ	Ⓒ

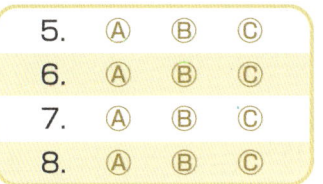

5 Why does the boy have a bad headache?

(A) He was jumping too high.

(B) A book fell on his head.

(C) He fell off the ladder.

6 What does the girl remember to do?

(A) Bring the janitor towels

(B) Clean the desks

(C) Go to the office

7 How will the boy get water?

(A) By buying a bottle of water

(B) From the fountain in the hallway

(C) By getting water from the sink

8 What does the girl want to do?

(A) Make a tall building

(B) Build a house like hers

(C) Put away the building blocks

書き取り

ミニテスト

Listen to *Mini Test* again. Write the correct word in each blank.
(ミニテストをもう一度聞き，＿＿＿にあてはまる単語を書きましょう。)

1. W: Our art project today is to make a clay cup.
   G: Can I make a bowl ¹i_____ _____ a cup, please?
   W: ²_____ d_____ t_____ that is a good idea.
   G: Please, I think it would turn out really well.

2. M: Today we are going to run around the track four times.
   B: Oh, I didn't know we were doing that today. I'll switch my shoes.
   M: Why do you need to do that?
   B: Because the shoes I'm wearing are ³n_____ f_____ r_____.

3. W: Are you ⁴l_____ f_____ something? Do you need my help?
   G: I need to find a video and a book on farm animals.
   W: Oh, well I see you found a book about farm animals.
   G: Yes, I did. Now I just need to find a video ⁵_____ t_____ s_____ t_____.
   W: We keep all videos in the video room. If you can't find it, just come to me again.

4. G1: Are you ready for our English test tomorrow?
   G2: No, are you?
   G1: Yeah, but I can't understand the review handout. Do you get it?
   G2: Not really, I think it's really hard. Do you want to ⁶s_____ t_____ tonight?
   G1: Yes, that would be great.

5 W: So tell me, why do you have such a bad headache?
B: I was trying to reach up and get a book on the top shelf.
W: Let me guess. You accidently knocked down several books.
B: Yes, many books fell, and one really big book ⁷h_____ _____ h_____.
W: I can see that from the bump on the back of your head. Let's ⁸p_____ some i_____ _____ _____.

6 M: Thank you for bringing me these paper towels.
G: You're welcome. My teacher reminded me to after class. She said you needed them as soon as possible.
M: Good, I'm glad you did that. It's always nice to talk to students.
G: I'd like to say thank you for all you do for our school. You ⁹k_____ everything _____ c_____!
M: Of course, that's my job. And I really like that you care.

7 W: Now, let's open our books to page seven and ¹⁰b_____ r_____.
B: Before we start reading, may I please get a drink of water out in the hallway? I am very thirsty.
W: Oh, you can use the sink in the classroom to get water. But please be quick.
B: OK, thank you.
W: Be sure to use a paper cup to drink the water.

8 M: I like how neatly you can stack all of the building blocks together.
G: Thank you. I really like playing with the building blocks. They are ¹¹f_____ _____ p_____ w_____.
M: You should ¹²t_____ m_____ a tall building with them. Like the buildings outside of the school.
G: Hmm, I think I would rather build a house that looks exactly like mine.
M: Oh that's a brilliant idea. I'm sure it will be really fun to build.

Lesson 13   119

Lesson 14　What will she do next?

▶ 問題の形式

このセクションでは，2人の日常会話を聞きます。最も正しい答えを選びましょう。選択肢は3つあります。

> **ヒント**
> ・親，兄弟姉妹，店員さんたち，お医者さんたちなどとの会話が流れます。
> ・会話が流れる前に，質問文と選択肢にさっと目を通しておきましょう。それから会話を聞き取り，関連する情報を探しましょう。
> ・聞き取りながら，間違っていると思う選択肢があれば，外していきましょう。

Example

CD1 16 Listen to a conversation and answer a question.
（会話を聞いて，問題に答えましょう。）

1 Why will they go to the park?

(A) To play soccer outside
(B) To get the girl's shoes
(C) To go on the playground

2 What will the girl do next?

(A) Take off her hat
(B) Put on some earrings
(C) Try on the gold necklace

Script

1. B: It's so sunny outside!
   G: I really want to play soccer.
   B: Oh, that's a great idea. Let's go to the park to play.
   G: OK, I will get my soccer ball and shoes.

2. W: Would you like to see any of our necklaces?
   G: Yes, that gold one with pink jewels please.
   W: Oh that one is lovely. Can I help you put it on?
   G: Yes, that would be very helpful.

Answer

1. 答え　(A)

   これはきょうだいの間の会話です。男の子がよい天気だと言い，女の子がサッカーがしたいと言います。男の子は Let's go to the park to play.（公園に行ってサッカーをしよう）と言います。したがって質問の答えは，(A) To play soccer outside.（外でサッカーをする）です。

2. 答え　(C)

   これは宝石店で店員と女性がしている会話です。女性は，ピンクの宝石のついた金のネックレスがほしいと言い，店員は女性がそれを着けてみる（試着する）のを手伝おうとしました。したがって質問の答えは，(C) Try on the gold necklace（金のネックレスを着けてみる）です。

重要ポイント

- **It seems like ~**　　～みたいだ

  It seems like a dream.
  It seems like a holiday.

  やってみよう！

  It seems like ＿＿＿＿＿ ＿＿＿＿＿ ＿＿＿＿＿ .

  よい考えのようです。

- **There is nothing to ~**　　～するものは何もない

  There is nothing to drink in the refrigerator.
  There is nothing to worry about.

  やってみよう！

  There is nothing to ＿＿＿＿＿ ＿＿＿＿＿ .

  遊ぶもの（道具）が何もありません。

練習問題

Listen to a conversation and answer a question.
（会話を聞いて，問題に答えましょう。）

1 What does the son want to do?

(A) Watch a funny movie
(B) Buy some candy for the movie
(C) See a scary movie with his mom

2 How did the girl break her leg?

(A) She was jumping rope after school.
(B) She was riding her bike and fell off.
(C) She was climbing a tree and fell.

3 What will the girl do next?

(A) Ask for her shoe size
(B) Try on the shoes
(C) Go for a run

4 What does the boy agree to do?

(A) Write a letter to his neighbor
(B) Give the package to his neighbor
(C) Help the mail carrier find his neighbor

NOTE

- a scary movie: 怖い映画
- frightened: 怖がって
- would rather ~: （…ではなくて）むしろ〜したい

- result:（検査の）結果
- a pretty big tree: かなり大きい（高い）木
- jump rope: なわとびをする

- cool: かっこいい
- comfortable: 楽だ
- agree: 同じ意見だ
- hand: 手渡す

- mail carrier: 郵便配達員
- neighbor: おとなりさん
- package: 小包

5 Why does the boy buy the hat?

　(A)　To play with it
　(B)　To keep it for himself
　(C)　To give it to his friend

> NOTE
> ・look good on: 〜に似合う
> ・look for 〜: 〜を探す
> ・discount: 値引き

6 What will the daughter do next?

　(A)　Take a rest
　(B)　Go to a movie
　(C)　Play with her friends

・hang out with 〜: 〜と仲よくする
・take a rest: 休む，休息を取る

7 How will the girl get home?

　(A)　She will take the subway home.
　(B)　She will walk the rest of the way.
　(C)　The bus driver will bring her to her house.

・nap: 居眠り，昼寝
・tiring: 疲れさせる（骨の折れる）
・drop off:（車から）下ろす
・don't mind walking: 歩くのは平気だ（気にしない）

8 Why does the boy want ice skates?

　(A)　To play with his friends
　(B)　To go ice skating with his sister
　(C)　To give them to his sister for her birthday

・the perfect time of year: 1年のうちで最もよい時期
・spend time with 〜: 〜といっしょに時を過ごす

Lesson 14

ミニテスト

Listen to a conversation and answer a question. Fill in the correct circles on your answer sheet.
（会話を聞いて，解答欄の正しい丸をぬりつぶしましょう。）

1. Ⓐ Ⓑ Ⓒ
2. Ⓐ Ⓑ Ⓒ
3. Ⓐ Ⓑ Ⓒ
4. Ⓐ Ⓑ Ⓒ

1 What does the brother want?

(A) A napkin to clean the table
(B) More ice cream in his cup
(C) A spoon to eat his ice cream with

2 Where is the store?

(A) On the left of the street corner
(B) On the right of the street corner
(C) On the left side of the house

3 Why does the girl color?

(A) To help time go by
(B) To finish her homework
(C) To help the waiter

4 Where will the father and son go next?

(A) To the art museum
(B) To the football game
(C) To the baseball field

5.	Ⓐ	Ⓑ	Ⓒ
6.	Ⓐ	Ⓑ	Ⓒ
7.	Ⓐ	Ⓑ	Ⓒ
8.	Ⓐ	Ⓑ	Ⓒ

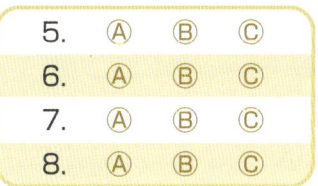

5 What does the boy agree to do?

 (A) Follow the vet's advice
 (B) Give the puppy medicine
 (C) Bring his puppy to the park

6 What does the boy want to do?

 (A) Drink orange juice
 (B) Make sandwiches
 (C) Bake cookies

7 What will the girl do next?

 (A) Draw a picture of the man
 (B) Tell what the man looked like
 (C) Find the watch that was stolen

8 What does the boy want?

 (A) Chicken nuggets
 (B) A large amount of food
 (C) A grilled cheese sandwich

書き取り

ミニテスト

Listen to *Mini Test* again. Write the correct word in each blank.
(ミニテストをもう一度聞き，_____にあてはまる単語を書きましょう。)

1 B: How come I have so much ice cream?
   G: Because you asked for two big scoops instead of one.
   B: Oh that's ¹t_____ m_____ f_____ _____. Now, I need a spoon to eat it.
   G: I think you might need a couple of napkins too!

2 W: Oh no, I ran out of milk for our cookies. Can you ²r_____ _____ t_____ s_____ and buy milk?
   G: I would love to, but I don't know where the store is.
   W: It's not too far from here. Just walk to the street corner. It's on the left.
   G: ³A_____ y_____ s_____ it's on the left side?
   W: Of course, you will see the store.

3 M: Welcome to Denny's Restaurant. Would you like a coloring sheet and crayons while you wait for a table?
   G: Thank you, I love to color.
   M: No problem, waiting is very boring sometimes.
   G: Yes, the restaurant looks very busy today.
   M: Don't worry. Coloring will make ⁴t_____ t_____ _____ _____ f_____.
   G: I hope so.

4 M: I can't believe it's still ⁵r_____ o_____.
   B: I hate rain. I really wanted to play baseball today.
   M: Oh wait, I think the sky is clearing up!
   B: Awesome. Let's go to the baseball field.
   M: ⁶S_____ g_____, I will get the baseball bat and gloves.

5 M: Your puppy is just sick. There is nothing to worry about.

B: Oh thank you, I ⁷w_____ s_____ there was something terribly wrong.

M: You just need to give your puppy a rest and some water to drink.

B: That sounds good. I will surely do that.

6 G: This orange juice tastes delicious. Do you want to ⁸t_____ s_____?

B: No thanks. I am really hungry though. I wish we had some bread and ham.

G: Why do you want bread and ham?

B: I want to make my famous ham sandwich!

G: That sounds better than my orange juice. I am ⁹g_____ h_____ now.

7 M: Hey, did you by chance see who stole that watch from the shelf?

G: I think so. He looked like an old grandpa with gray hair and big ears.

M: Can you tell my friend what he looked like? She will draw a picture of him.

G: Sure, I can try and remember all the details of what he looked like.

M: Thank you. That would be very helpful in order to ¹⁰s_____ o_____ c_____.

8 W: Hello. Would you like to see our kids' menu? The serving sizes are smaller.

B: That's good. I cannot eat ¹¹_____ m_____ _____ my mom and dad.

W: Here is the kids' menu. What would you like to ¹²o_____?

B: I think I will have the grilled cheese sandwich and French fries.

W: Oh really? Our chicken nuggets are the best thing on the kids' menu.

B: But I would like to eat cheese today, and I really like sandwiches.

Lesson 14   **127**

Listening Part 5

Unit 10

Short Messages
（短いメッセージ）

❯ Lesson 15   Why did he call?

❯ Lesson 16   What is he talking about?

Lesson 15 Why did he call?

▶ 問題の形式

このセクションでは，短い電話メッセージを聞いて，電話の目的やどうしてほしいのかを考えます。最も正しい答えを選びましょう。
選択肢は3つあります。

> **ヒント**
> ・電話メッセージが流れる前に，質問文と答えの選択肢に目を通しておきましょう。
> ・電話メッセージはたいてい友達や先生からのものです。電話をしてメッセージを残した理由を考えましょう。
> ・細かい内容を問う質問の場合には，関連する情報をよく聞き取ってください。

Example

CD2-1 Listen to a message and answer a question.
（メッセージを聞いて，問題に答えましょう。）

1 Why did Tyler call?

(A) To ask for his book back
(B) To explain the reading book
(C) To decide where to meet tomorrow

Script
F: Hey, Steve. It's Tyler. I forgot my book at your house. Can you bring it to school with you tomorrow? I will get it from you then.

2 What did the father call about?

(A) A school trip
(B) The movie time
(C) The movie theater

Script
F: Hi, it's Dad. I'd like to know what time the movie starts. Please call me back, so I know what time I should be at the movie theater. Thanks.

Answer

1. 答え　(A)

このメッセージは，タイラーがスティーブの家に本を忘れたので，明日学校に持って来るように頼んでいます。したがって質問の答えは，(A) To ask for his book back（本を返すように頼むため）です。

2. 答え　(B)

このメッセージはお父さんからで，映画が何時に始まるか聞いています。したがって質問の答えは，(B) The movie time（映画の時刻）です。

重要ポイント

- **Can you bring ~?**　～を持って来られませんか，～を持って来てください

  Can you bring your family picture?
  Can you bring your dog to the park?

  やってみよう！
  Can you bring _____ to _____ _____ ?
  ピクニックにソーダを持って来てください。

- **Remember to ~**　～するよう覚えておいてください，忘れないで～してください

  Remember to close the window.
  Remember to water the flowers.

  やってみよう！
  Remember to _____ _____ _____ .
  忘れずに傘を持って行ってください。

練習問題

Listen to a message and answer a question.
（メッセージを聞いて，問題に答えましょう。）

1 Why did Jenny call?

- (A)　To explain a fun game
- (B)　To talk about the weather
- (C)　To invite Sam to play outside

2 Why did Jake call?

- (A)　To ask Carl for help
- (B)　To tell Carl where the library is
- (C)　To tell Carl about the math test

3 Why did the teacher call?

- (A)　To invite Ji-hu to the zoo
- (B)　To tell Ji-hu to bring his toy
- (C)　To ask about the guest speaker

4 Why did Ben call?

- (A)　To talk about his friends
- (B)　To borrow a sleeping bag
- (C)　To invite Luke to go camping

NOTE

- make a snowman：雪だるまを作る
- explain：説明する

- have trouble with ~：～で困ったことがある

- guest speaker：ゲストスピーカー（外部から呼んだ先生），特別講師
- stuffed animal：ぬいぐるみ（の動物）

- a few friends：何人かの友達
- sleeping bag：寝袋
- borrow：借りる

5 What did the grandmother call about?

- (A) Susan's jacket
- (B) Susan's school
- (C) House cleaning

6 What does the teacher want from Ryan?

- (A) His signed test
- (B) His reading book
- (C) His writing paper

7 Why did John call?

- (A) To tell Kyle to bring some snacks
- (B) To invite Kyle to play at the park
- (C) To ask about the new playground

8 Why did Scott call?

- (A) To explain how to rock climb
- (B) To sing at his birthday party
- (C) To invite Paul to eat pizza

NOTE

· drop off at ~
: ～に届ける

· sign: 署名する

· after school: 放課後に

· rock climbing: ロッククライミング

ミニテスト

**Listen to a message and answer a question.
Fill in the correct circles on your answer sheet.**
（メッセージを聞いて，解答欄の正しい丸をぬりつぶしましょう。）

1. Ⓐ Ⓑ Ⓒ
2. Ⓐ Ⓑ Ⓒ
3. Ⓐ Ⓑ Ⓒ
4. Ⓐ Ⓑ Ⓒ

1 Why did the mother call?

(A) To ask where to buy flowers
(B) To explain how to water flowers
(C) To tell Kayla to clean the windows

2 Why did Gina call?

(A) To talk about the new violin song
(B) To tell Rachel to bring her violin
(C) To ask to practice together

3 What did Ashley call about?

(A) Tennis practice
(B) The nice old coach
(C) The new tennis coach

4 Why did the teacher call?

(A) To tell Billy to bring a form to school
(B) To explain the field trip program
(C) To talk about the school project

5.	Ⓐ	Ⓑ	Ⓒ
6.	Ⓐ	Ⓑ	Ⓒ
7.	Ⓐ	Ⓑ	Ⓒ
8.	Ⓐ	Ⓑ	Ⓒ

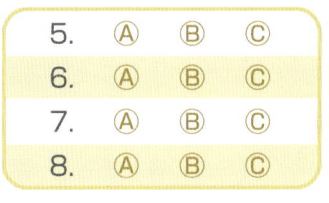

5 **What did Lucy lose?**

(A) Her backpack

(B) Her sketchbook

(C) Her science project

6 **What did the grandfather get at the store?**

(A) Milk

(B) A table

(C) Cookies

7 **What does Anna want?**

(A) To go to a different school

(B) To ride the bus with Michelle

(C) To walk to school with Michelle

8 **What is Amy keeping for Stephanie?**

(A) Her library book

(B) Her homework

(C) Her backpack

書き取り

ミニテスト

Listen to *Mini Test* again. Write the correct word in each blank.
(ミニテストをもう一度聞き，＿＿にあてはまる単語を書きましょう。)

1 W: Hi, Kayla. It's Mom. Please ¹r_____ _____ w_____ the flowers by the window. Use one cup of water and don't pour it in too fast. Thanks.

2 G: Hi, Rachel. This is Gina from music class. I need help playing the new violin song we learned today. Can I ²s_____ _____ y_____ tomorrow, so I can ³p_____ w_____ y_____?

3 G: Hey, Jane. It's Ashley. I am ⁴c_____ a_____ our new tennis coach. Do you like him? I think the new coach is kind of mean. But maybe it's because our old coach was so nice. I want to hear ⁵w_____ y_____ t_____.

4 M: Hello, Billy. This is your teacher, Mr. Smith. The school field trip is next week. You need a permission form from your parents. Please ⁶b_____ _____ w_____ y_____ to school tomorrow. If you don't, you can't go on the field trip.

5 G: Hi, Chloe. It's Lucy. Are you tired? I'm really tired now. I think it's because we were working on the art project for so long. By the way, I couldn't find my sketchbook ⁷a_____ _____ c_____ h_____. Can you ⁸l_____ a_____ in your room? Please tell me if it's there.

6 M: Hi, Jake. It's your grandfather. I stopped at the store quickly to buy some milk, so you can have milk and cookies ⁹f_____ _____ s_____. When you get to the house, please start doing your homework at the table. I will be back soon.

7 G: Good morning, Michelle. It's Anna calling. My old friend rides a different school bus than me now because she ¹⁰g_____ _____ a_____ s_____. My mom thinks it's safer if I have a friend to ride the bus with. So can I ride the bus with you, starting today? Do you think that would be OK?

8 G: Hello, Stephanie. This is Amy. I called because you left your backpack in the library. But don't worry about it because I'm ¹¹k_____ _____ f_____ y_____. I have lots of homework to do, so my mom said she can bring it to you. Call me back when you ¹²g_____ h_____.

Lesson 15   137

Lesson 16 — What is he talking about?

▶ **問題の形式**

このセクションでは，学校の連絡事項を聞きます。最も正しい答えを選びましょう。選択肢は3つあります。

ヒント
- リスニングが始まる前に，まず質問文と答えの選択肢を読んでください。
- 連絡は，学校の校長先生や先生からのものがほとんどです。連絡事項の内容を理解しましょう。
- 連絡事項の細かい点をよく聞き取ってください。

Example

Listen to a message and answer a question.
（よく聞いて，問題に答えましょう。）

1 Why do the students need a library card?

(A) To buy books
(B) To find books
(C) To borrow books

Script
W: When you want to check out books, come up to the front desk. Bring your library card and show it to the person at the desk.

2 What is the teacher talking about?

(A) How to walk silently
(B) Going outside to play
(C) Being quiet in the hallway

Script
W: When we walk down the hallway, please be quiet. Do not talk loudly and try to walk silently. Let's not make any noise.

Answer

1. 答え　(C)
   これは図書館員から生徒に向けた連絡です。本を借りるには，図書館カードを持って行かなければなりません。したがって質問の答えは，(C) To borrow books（本を借りるため）です。

2. 答え　(C)
   これは先生から生徒たちへの連絡です。先生は，廊下を歩くときには静かにして，大声で話をしてはいけないと言っています。したがって質問の答えは，(C) Being quiet in the hallway（廊下では静かにすること）です。

重要ポイント

- **Let's not ~**　～しないでおこう

  Let's not run in the hallway.
  Let's not play in this neighborhood.

  やってみよう！
  Let's not ＿＿＿＿＿＿＿ ＿＿＿＿＿＿＿ at night.
  夜には何も食べないようにしよう。

- **enjoy ~ing**　～することを楽しむ

  I **enjoy** danc**ing** with my sister.
  Mom **enjoys** talk**ing** to the lady next door.

  やってみよう！
  We **enjoy** ＿＿＿＿＿＿＿ ＿＿＿＿＿＿＿ ＿＿＿＿＿＿＿.
  私たちは，音楽を聞くのを楽しみます。

練習問題

CD2 5 Listen to a message and answer a question.
（よく聞いて，問題に答えましょう。）

1 What is the principal talking about?

(A) An event for the second grade class
(B) Parents visiting the school
(C) The story of the play

NOTE
- the second grade: 2年生
- play: 演劇

2 What is the teacher talking about?

(A) The sunny weather
(B) School ending early
(C) Calling the parents

- because of ~: ～のため
- pick up:（乗せるために）迎えに来る

3 What is the principal talking about?

(A) Learning how to dance
(B) How to win a game
(C) A school event

- school dance: 学校のダンスパーティー
- get a prize: 賞品をもらう
- have fun: 楽しむ（楽しく過ごす）

4 What is the principal asking the students to do?

(A) To sign up for the contest
(B) To take a trip to a big city
(C) To practice spelling words

- sign up: 申し込む
- main office: 事務室
- grand prize: 最優秀賞

5 What should the baseball players do in the gym?

(A) Play catch
(B) Practice running
(C) Pick up baseballs

NOTE
- thunder: 雷（の音）
- baseball: 野球のボール
- gym: 体育館
- play catch: キャッチボールをする

6 What is the teacher talking about?

(A) The story of the golden lion
(B) What pages to read in the book
(C) What they did yesterday in class

- miss: 逃す（見聞きする事ができない）
- quietly: 静かに
- by yourself: 自分ひとりで

7 What does the teacher ask the students to do?

(A) Bring materials for class
(B) Draw a flower in a pot
(C) Plant a flower outside

- plant: 植える
- every year: 毎年（年ごとに）
- material: 材料（教材）

8 What is the coach talking about?

(A) Changing the practice schedule
(B) A basketball game
(C) A new member

- get to know: 知るようになる
- practice schedule: 練習計画

Lesson 16　141

ミニテスト

Listen to a message and answer a question.
Fill in the correct circles on your answer sheet.
（よく聞いて，解答欄の正しい丸をぬりつぶしましょう。）

1. Ⓐ Ⓑ Ⓒ
2. Ⓐ Ⓑ Ⓒ
3. Ⓐ Ⓑ Ⓒ
4. Ⓐ Ⓑ Ⓒ

1 What is the principal talking about?

(A) The books in the library
(B) The school book fair
(C) Buying books online

2 What is the principal talking about?

(A) A school holiday
(B) Families going camping
(C) Activities for family night

3 How can students borrow the magazines?

(A) By writing their names down
(B) By ordering the magazines
(C) By telling the librarian

4 What is the teacher talking about?

(A) Everyone's birthdays
(B) How to cook cupcakes
(C) Bringing drinks to class

5.	Ⓐ	Ⓑ	Ⓒ
6.	Ⓐ	Ⓑ	Ⓒ
7.	Ⓐ	Ⓑ	Ⓒ
8.	Ⓐ	Ⓑ	Ⓒ

5 Why does Sam join the track team?

(A) To win medals

(B) To run outside

(C) To meet friends

6 What is the coach talking about?

(A) His basketball coach

(B) His basketball life

(C) His children

7 What is the principal talking about?

(A) Scary stories

(B) A Halloween parade

(C) Halloween costumes

8 What is the principal talking about?

(A) How to keep from getting sick

(B) How early the class will end

(C) How to stay warm in school

書き取り

ミニテスト

Listen to *Mini Test* again. Write the correct word in each blank.
(ミニテストをもう一度聞き，_____にあてはまる単語を書きましょう。)

1. M: On Wednesday, we will have a book fair. At a book fair, you can ¹l_____ _____ all different kinds of books. And you can buy the books that you like.

2. W: Please invite your mom, dad, sisters, and brothers to our family fun night this Friday. We will have lots of ²t_____ _____ _____ like games, watch movies, and even watch a play!

3. W: We just ordered some new magazines today. If you want to read them, please write your name ³_____ t_____ p_____ hanging on the wall. Then I will know ⁴w_____ _____ s_____ g_____ the magazines to first.

4. M: Mary's birthday is tomorrow. She is going to bring cupcakes to ⁵s_____ w_____ everyone. I want each of you to bring your own drink. You could bring juice, milk, or water. We can celebrate Mary's birthday after story time.

5 M: I would like to introduce the new runner to our team. This is Sam, and he was the fastest runner at his old school. He ⁶w_____ _____ j_____ our track team to meet new friends. So please, ⁷w_____ s_____ by saying hello and introducing yourselves.

6 M: Hello everyone. I am the new basketball coach ⁸t_____ y_____. I started playing basketball 20 years ago. I was a very good player until I broke my ankle last year. I ⁹e_____ t_____ basketball to young kids. It is a great sport to play.

7 W: Next Friday is Halloween! To celebrate you can wear a costume to school. For example, you can dress like a witch or a ghost. Your costume can be scary ¹⁰l_____ _____ m_____ or funny like a clown. But please, no fake blood. That can get messy, and it might scare some of the other students.

8 M: There are many students getting sick these days. I want you to be extra careful, so you don't ¹¹g_____ _____ c_____. Please wash your hands with soap and cover your mouth when you cough. And drink as much water or orange juice as you can. I don't want to see any more students going home in the middle of class because they ¹² _____ n_____ f_____ w_____.

模擬テスト

(第1回)

(実際のテストでは，CDのトラックナンバーを示すマークは入りません。)

Reading

Part 1

Look at the picture. Read the words. Which words go with the picture?
Fill in the correct circles on your answer sheet.

Let's do two examples.

1.

    (A)   Parrot
    (B)   Bat
    (C)   Chicken

The answer is "B." Fill in "B" on your answer sheet for question 1.

2.

    (A)   Both cats are eating fish.
    (B)   The black cat is thinner than the brown cat.
    (C)   The brown cat is fatter than the black cat.

The answer is "A." Fill in "A" on your answer sheet for question 2.

Go On

Reading

3.

- (A) Television
- (B) Phone
- (C) Camera

4.

- (A) Ant
- (B) Animal
- (C) Spider

Reading

5.

(A) Skirt
(B) Cap
(C) Blouse

6.

(A) Cut
(B) Grab
(C) Wash

Go On

Reading

7.

- (A) Cloudy
- (B) Snowy
- (C) Rainy

8.

- (A) Take off
- (B) Get on
- (C) Go on

Reading

9.

(A) Cold water
(B) Hot water
(C) Warm water

10.

(A) Bee
(B) Bird
(C) Board

Reading

11.

(A) He is eating a sandwich.

(B) The boy finished eating a sandwich.

(C) The boy eats a hamburger.

12.

(A) The girl is whispering to her friend.

(B) The girl is talking on the phone.

(C) The girl hangs up the phone.

Go On

Reading

13.

- (A) She reads a big book.
- (B) The woman is buying a newspaper.
- (C) The woman is reading a newspaper.

14.

- (A) All of them are the same shape.
- (B) The triangle is the smallest shape.
- (C) The circle is bigger than the square.

Go On

Reading

15.

- (A) The man is eating popcorn.
- (B) The woman is watching television.
- (C) He is sitting on a sofa.

16.

- (A) There are two apples on the table.
- (B) The grapes are the biggest in the group.
- (C) The orange is next to the apple.

Go On

Reading

17.

- (A) He went to bed very late.
- (B) The boy wakes up early in the morning.
- (C) It is 10 o'clock in the morning.

18.

- (A) She is drawing on the wall.
- (B) The girl likes to write a letter.
- (C) She is painting a picture.

Reading

Part 2

Read and find the answer.
Fill in the correct circles on your answer sheet.

Let's do an example.

19. It is a place. You go here when you travel. You ride a plane here.

    It is a(n) _____ .

    (A) airport
    (B) station
    (C) train

    The answer is "A." Fill in "A" on your answer sheet for question 19.

---

20. It is sweet. It is a type of food. There is a hole in the middle of it.

    What is it?

    (A) A cone
    (B) A donut
    (C) A tire

21. The opposite is hard. A cat's fur feels like this. It can also feel smooth.

    What is it?

    (A) Rough
    (B) Soft
    (C) Different

Go On

Reading

22. Dogs do this with bones. People do this when they are looking for treasure.

What are they doing?

(A) Singing
(B) Climbing
(C) Digging

23. You do this when you make a picture. You do this on your notebook. You can do it with color.

What are you doing?

(A) Clapping
(B) Drawing
(C) Lifting

24. You go here to see history. You go here to see art. You can also go here on a field trip.

Where are you going?

(A) A park
(B) A theater
(C) A museum

25. It is a color. It is bright. The sun looks like this.

What is it?

(A) Yellow
(B) Blue
(C) Black

Go On

Reading

26. It is an area of grass on a farm. You can find corn here. You can also find rice.

    What is it?

    (A) A ground
    (B) A field
    (C) A pool

27. This day is very noisy outside. It is not calm. The leaves are blowing.

    The day is _____.

    (A) windy
    (B) sunny
    (C) cool

Reading

Go On

Reading

Part 3

Fill in the correct circles on your answer sheet.
Read the invitation. Then answer questions 28 to 31.

Please Join the Graduation Party for......

Hannah Meyer!!

And her fellow 6th grade friends

Saturday, May 25th at 2 p.m.

Hannah's Home
210 29th Ave

Respond to Cathy (Hannah's Mom) 701-334-2222

Reading

28. You want to go to the party. You should call _____.

    (A) Hannah

    (B) Hannah's father

    (C) Hannah's mother

29. Who is the party for?

    (A) Only Hannah

    (B) Hannah and her mom

    (C) Hannah and her classmates

30. Where is the party?

    (A) School

    (B) Hannah's home

    (C) A restaurant

31. When is the party?

    (A) Sunday

    (B) Saturday

    (C) Holiday

Reading

Read the poster. Then answer questions 32 to 35.

Come Visit Happy Zoo!

New Schedule for Kids on Saturdays

Event	Time	Place
See Lions Do Tricks	11 AM	Lion's Den
Take Pictures With Monkeys	12 PM	Monkey House
Drawing With Penguins	1 PM	Penguin Place
Watch a Dolphin Show	2 PM	The Aquarium

Office Hours are 9:00 AM to 7:00 PM Monday Through Friday

Go On

Reading

32. When is the event?

    (A) Monday

    (B) Friday

    (C) Saturday

33. What time do the events start?

    (A) 9 AM

    (B) 11 PM

    (C) 11 AM

34. If you want to see a dolphin show, you can go to _____.

    (A) the aquarium

    (B) the penguin place

    (C) the monkey house

35. When can you take a picture with monkeys?

    (A) 11 AM

    (B) 12 PM

    (C) 1 PM

Go On

Reading

Read the letter. Then answer questions 36 and 37.

Dear Mom,

You are the best cook in the whole world! The cookies you baked last week were the best. I liked the chocolate chip cookies the most! I shared all of the cookies with my friends in class. Even our teacher wants you to bake them again. Everyone loved them so much. Maybe next time we can bake them together. You can teach me how to make these delicious cookies.

Love,
Tanya

---

36. What does Tanya want?

(A) To eat more cookies
(B) To bake cookies together with her mom
(C) Her mom to always bake cookies

37. Who is writing the letter?

(A) Tanya's mother
(B) Tanya's teacher
(C) Tanya

Reading

Read the text. Then answer questions 38 and 39.

Have you ever been to a hotel on a trip? I bet you've never been to an ice hotel! In Canada, there is an ice hotel. Everything is ice inside the hotel and it is open only during the winter. There are many things to do in the hotel. There is a restaurant and you can eat from ice cups and plates. Even your spoon is ice. Have you ever slept on the snow? Well at this hotel, you can sleep on an ice bed!

38. What is this text about?

   (A) About an ice hotel
   (B) About Canada
   (C) About a trip

39. What is not in the hotel?

   (A) A restaurant
   (B) A swimming pool
   (C) Ice beds

STOP

You finished the reading test.

Listening

Part 1

Listen to the sentence. Look at the pictures.
Fill in the correct circles on your answer sheet.

Let's do an example.

1.

(A)    (B)    (C)

The answer is "B." Fill in "B" on your answer sheet for question 1.

Now, you do it.

2.

(A) 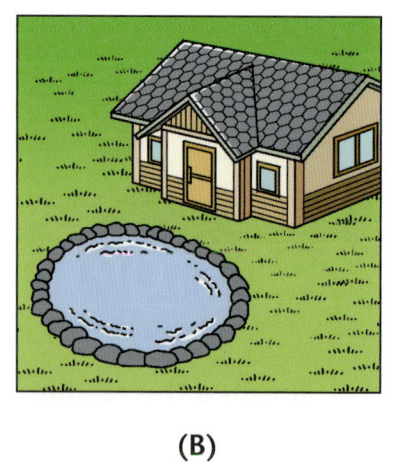   (B)    (C)

Go On

Listening

3.

(A)  (B)  (C)

4.

(A)  (B)  (C)

5.

(A)  (B)  (C)

Go On

Listening

6.

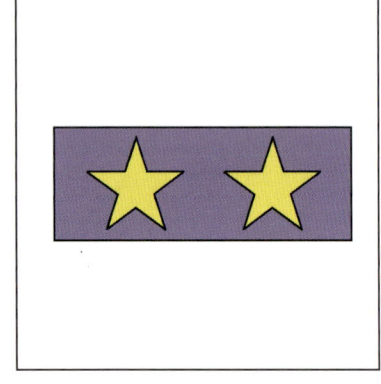

(A) 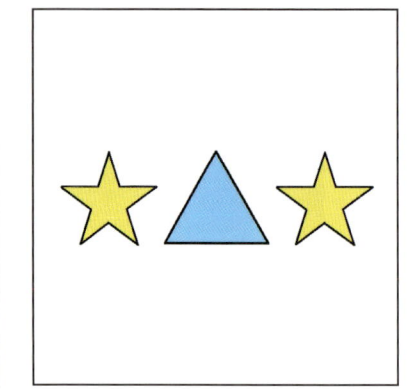　(B) 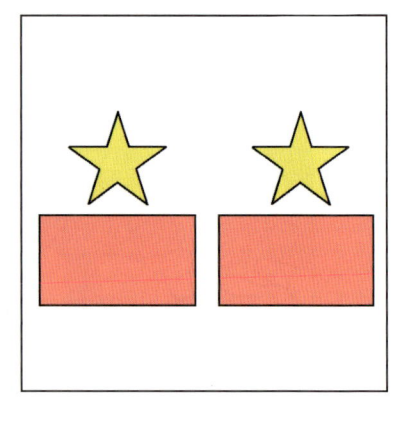　(C)

7.

(A) 　(B) 　(C)

8.

|  Kim Ben Jack |  Jack Kim Ben |  Kim Jack Ben |
| (A) | (B) | (C) |

170

Go On

Listening

Part 2 [CD2 16]

Listen to the sentences. Look at the pictures.
Fill in the correct circles on your answer sheet.

Let's do an example.

9. Listen to a teacher. What did the teacher tell the students to do?

(A)    (B)    (C)

The answer is "A." Fill in "A" on your answer sheet for question 9.

Now, you do it.

---

10. [CD2 17]

(A)    (B)    (C)

171

Go On

Listening

11.

(A) 　　　(B) 　　　(C)

12.

(A) 　　　(B) 　　　(C)

13.

(A) 　　　(B) 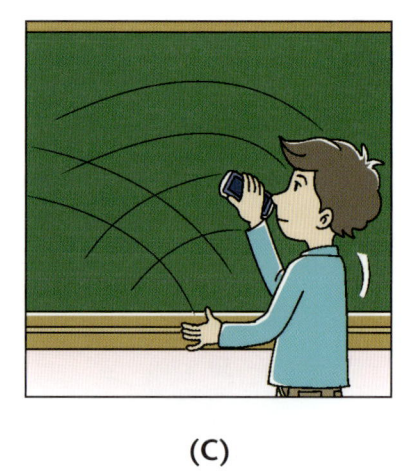　　　(C)

Listening

14.

(A)    (B)    (C)

15.

(A)    (B)    (C)

16.

(A)    (B)    (C)

Go On

Listening

17.

(A)    (B)    (C)

18.

(A)    (B)    (C)

19.

(A)    (B)    (C)

Go On

Listening

Part 3

Fill in the correct circles on your answer sheet.

Let's do an example.

20. Look at your answer sheet for Part 3. Listen to the conversations. Which conversation sounds correct?

The answer is "B." Fill in "B" on your answer sheet for question 20.

Now, you do it.

Look at your answer sheet for questions 21 to 29.

Go On

Listening

Part 4

Listen to a conversation and answer a question.
Fill in the correct circles on your answer sheet.

Let's do an example.

30. What will the girl do next?

(A) Call her mom
(B) Go to the library
(C) Write in her notebook

The answer is "B." Fill in "B" on your answer sheet for question 30.

Now, you do it.

---

31. What will the boy do next?

(A) Help pick up the backpacks
(B) Carry the backpacks outside
(C) Put on his backpack to go home

32. How will the boy protect himself?

(A) By using his hands
(B) By wearing a mask
(C) By closing his eyes

Listening

33. Where will the daughter go next?

(A) To a shoe store
(B) To another dress store
(C) To her cousin's wedding

34. What will the girl do next?

(A) Buy the coat
(B) Borrow some money
(C) Ask her mom for money

35. Why does the girl need a cast?

(A) Because her head hurts
(B) Because she broke her arm
(C) Because she needs a bandage

Listening

Part 5

Listen and then answer a question.
Fill in the correct circles on your answer sheet.

Let's do an example.

36. Why did the mother call?

   (A) To ask about his school
   (B) To go to his cousin's house together
   (C) To tell Brian to come home after school

The answer is "C." Fill in "C" on your answer sheet for question 36.

Now, you do it.

---

37. What did Pat call about?

   (A) Comic books
   (B) A comedy
   (C) A letter from an old friend

38. What should Marsha bring tomorrow?

   (A) A camera
   (B) Her lunch
   (C) Juice boxes

Go On

Listening

39. What is the teacher going to do?

    (A) Talk about wild animals

    (B) Finish the book today

    (C) Give extra homework

40. What is the principal asking the students to do?

    (A) To play at the game

    (B) To cheer at the game

    (C) To give the players food

41. What did Mary call about?

    (A) Riding the bus together

    (B) The new house on the corner

    (C) How pretty the new member is

You finished the listening test.

模擬テスト

（第2回）

（実際のテストでは，CDのトラックナンバーを示すマークは入りません。）

No test questions on this page

Reading

Part 1

Look at the picture. Read the words. Which words go with the picture?
Fill in the correct circles on your answer sheet.

Let's do two examples.

1.

(A) Dolphin
(B) Shark
(C) Octopus

The answer is "A." Fill in "A" on your answer sheet for question 1.

2.

(A) She likes the violin.
(B) The boy is playing the cello.
(C) He is playing the violin.

The answer is "C." Fill in "C" on your answer sheet for question 2.

Go On

Reading

3.

- (A) Frog
- (B) Duck
- (C) Dog

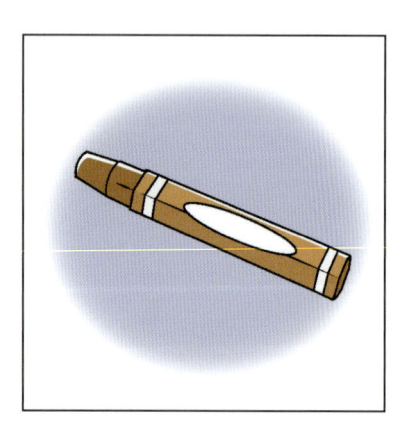

4.

- (A) Brown
- (B) Yellow
- (C) White

Reading

5.

- (A) Fork
- (B) Spoon
- (C) Knife

6.

- (A) Tomato
- (B) Onion
- (C) Pumpkin

Go On

Reading

7.

- (A) Bicycle
- (B) Car
- (C) Taxi

8.

- (A) Square pie
- (B) Round pie
- (C) Triangle pie

Go On

Reading

9.

- (A) Full box
- (B) Empty box
- (C) Blue box

10.

- (A) Smell
- (B) Talk
- (C) Watch

Go On

Reading

11.

- (A) The boy is washing his face.
- (B) He is brushing his teeth.
- (C) He is drinking water.

12.

- (A) The boy is catching a ball.
- (B) The ball is flying over the wall.
- (C) He is throwing a ball.

Go On

Reading

13.

- (A) There are many trees.
- (B) There are leaves under the tree.
- (C) The tree has many leaves.

14.

- (A) The three cups are the same size.
- (B) The pink cup is next to the red cup.
- (C) The red cup is the smallest cup.

Reading

15.

- (A) He is nodding his head.
- (B) The girl is shaking her head.
- (C) She is shaking her hand.

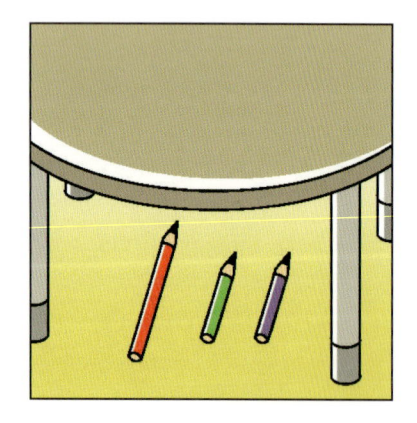

16.

- (A) The red pencil is the longest pencil.
- (B) The three pencils are on the table.
- (C) The green pencil is longer than the red pencil.

Reading

17.

- (A) She is cooking in the kitchen.
- (B) He is using a pot.
- (C) The man is holding a pan.

18.

- (A) The boy wants to be a scientist.
- (B) She is a scientist.
- (C) He wants to be a nurse.

Reading

Part 2

Read and find the answer.
Fill in the correct circles on your answer sheet.

Let's do an example.

19. It is a large area of water. Fish live here. It is surrounded by land.

    What is it?

    (A) A river
    (B) A lake
    (C) A mountain

    The answer is "B." Fill in "B" on your answer sheet for question 19.

---

20. This keeps you cool. It blows air on you. You use it during the summer.

    What is it?

    (A) A heater
    (B) A towel
    (C) A fan

21. You use this to eat. It goes with a spoon. It is usually made of metal.

    What is it?

    (A) A rock
    (B) A fork
    (C) A stick

Go On

Reading

22. This person is not strong. This person can't lift heavy things. This person is usually very thin.

    He is _____ .

    (A) weak
    (B) broad
    (C) worried

23. You need a pen or a pencil to do this. You do this to give an answer on a test. You do this on paper.

    What are you doing?

    (A) Making
    (B) Writing
    (C) Wearing

24. It is often yellow. Children ride it to school. It is very long.

    What is it?

    (A) A car
    (B) A taxi
    (C) A bus

25. You do this before you travel. You do this to make a schedule.

    You are making a(n) _____ .

    (A) shopping
    (B) object
    (C) plan

Reading

26. People do this when they buy something. People also do this when they go to a restaurant. They give money when they do this.

    What are they doing?

    (A) Paying
    (B) Stealing
    (C) Receiving

27. If you win the race, you are this. You need to be this to catch a chicken. You are not slow.

    You are _____.

    (A) quick
    (B) heavy
    (C) strange

Reading

Reading

Part 3

Fill in the correct circles on your answer sheet.
Read the sign. Then answer questions 28 to 31.

Welcome to Supermall!!

Where do you want to go?

Section A

- Food court
- Coffee shops
- Restaurants

Section B

- Clothing stores
- Sporting goods

Section C

- Game center
- Movie theater

Go On

Reading

28. Marlene is going on a hiking trip and needs shoes. Where should she go?

    (A) Section A
    (B) Section B
    (C) Section C

29. Tom is meeting his friends to see a movie. Where should he go?

    (A) Section A
    (B) Section B
    (C) Section C

30. Sandy is taking her brother out for dinner. Where should she go?

    (A) Section A
    (B) Section B
    (C) Section C

31. Joe needs shirts and jeans. Where should he go?

    (A) Section A
    (B) Section B
    (C) Section C

Go On

Reading

Read the handout. Then answer questions 32 to 35.

Parent's Day Schedule

9:00 AM	Arrive at the school with your kids
10:00 AM	Listen to the principal speak
11:00 AM	Lunchtime with all students
12:00 PM	Watch a school photo slideshow
1:00 PM	Go to the classroom
1:30 PM	Watch the teacher give a lesson
2:30 PM	Go home early with your children!

Reading

32. Where will the event be?

    (A) At school

    (B) At home

    (C) At sports center

33. When will they eat lunch?

    (A) 11:00 AM

    (B) 12:00 AM

    (C) 1:00 PM

34. Who is the handout for?

    (A) Teachers

    (B) Students

    (C) Parents

35. When will this event end?

    (A) 1:00 PM

    (B) 1:30 PM

    (C) 2:30 PM

Reading

Read the email. Then answer questions 36 and 37.

Dear students,

I want to remind you that your history reports are due this Friday. It is very important that you bring them to class on Friday. We will talk about each report in class on Friday. Also, I will be checking them over the weekend. I will minus points if you don't turn them in! So it is very important that you bring it. Work hard!

Your Teacher,
Mrs. Syndergaard

---

36. Why does the teacher write the email?

    (A) To tell her students about new homework
    (B) To give her students new homework
    (C) To remind her students to turn in the report

37. When is the homework due?

    (A) Friday
    (B) Monday
    (C) Weekend

Reading

Read the story. Then answer questions 38 and 39.

> Jonathan was very excited for his summer trip. He and his family were going to Europe. They were going to visit all the famous countries. He was most excited about France. He wanted to go to Paris to see the Eiffel Tower. Jonathan was also really excited to go to London. They were going to see Big Ben. Big Ben is a giant clock tower. Finally, his family was going to see Spain, Italy, and Germany. It would be a great trip for Jonathan.

38. What was Jonathan most excited about?

   (A) Big Ben
   (B) The Eiffel Tower
   (C) Spain

39. What is Big Ben?

   (A) A big clock tower
   (B) An old bell
   (C) A tall statue

STOP

You finished the reading test.

Listening

Part 1

Listen to the sentence. Look at the pictures.
Fill in the correct circles on your answer sheet.

(最後の問題まで，CDをとめずに答えましょう。)

Let's do an example.

1.

(A)　(B)　(C)

The answer is "A." Fill in "A" on your answer sheet for question 1.

Now, you do it.

2.

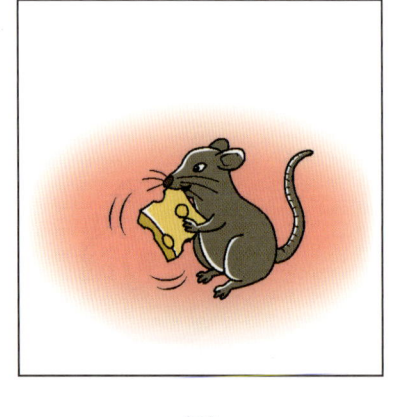

(A)　(B)　(C)

202

Go On

Listening

3.

(A)  (B)  (C)

4.

(A)  (B)  (C)

5.

(A)  (B)  (C)

203

Go On

Listening

6.

(A)    (B)    (C)

7.

(A)    (B)    (C)

8.

(A)    (B)    (C)

Listening

Part 2

Listen to the sentences. Look at the pictures.
Fill in the correct circles on your answer sheet.

Let's do an example.

9. Listen to a teacher. What did the teacher tell the student to do?

(A)   (B)   (C)

The answer is "C." Fill in "C" on your answer sheet for question 9.

Now, you do it.

10.

(A)   (B)   (C)

Go On

Listening

11.

(A)    (B)    (C)

12.

(A)    (B)    (C)

13.

(A)    (B)    (C)

Go On

Listening

14.

(A) 　(B) 　(C)

15.

(A) 　(B) 　(C)

16.

(A) 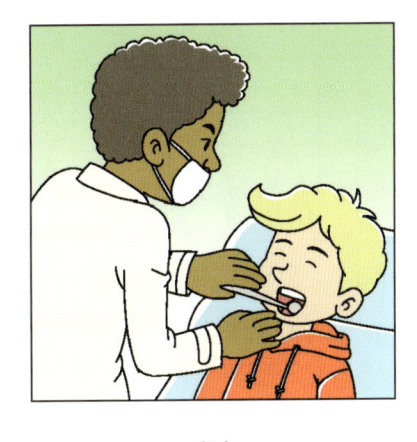　(B) 　(C)

Go On

Listening

17.

(A)  (B)  (C)

18.

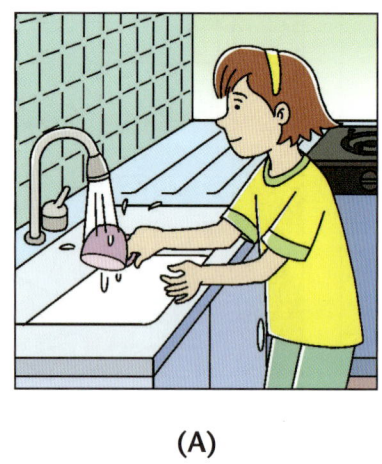

(A)  (B)  (C)

19.

(A)  (B)  (C)

Go On

Listening

Part 3

Fill in the correct circles on your answer sheet.

> Let's do an example.
>
> **20.** Look at your answer sheet for Part 3. Listen to the conversations. Which conversation sounds correct?
>
> The answer is "A." Fill in "A" on your answer sheet for question 20.
>
> Now, you do it.

Look at your answer sheet for questions 21 to 29.

Go On

Listening

Part 4

Listen to a conversation and answer a question.
Fill in the correct circles on your answer sheet.

Let's do an example.

30. What will the girl do next?

    (A) Study for the test
    (B) Listen to some music
    (C) Read a story to her class

The answer is "A." Fill in "A" on your answer sheet for question 30.

Now, you do it.

---

31. What does the boy agree to do?

    (A) Read a book
    (B) Memorize his lines
    (C) Practice his singing

32. What will the boy do next?

    (A) Read the directions
    (B) Turn on his computer
    (C) Plug in the power cord

Go On

Listening

33. What does the brother agree to do?

(A) Cut the cake
(B) Wear a birthday hat
(C) Blow out birthday candles

34. Why does the girl buy a swimsuit?

(A) For a pool party
(B) For her friend
(C) For her swimming lessons

35. What does the boy want to do?

(A) Whiten the dog's teeth
(B) Take his dog to the dentist
(C) Get his dog's teeth cleaned

Listening

Part 5

Listen and then answer a question.
Fill in the correct circles on your answer sheet.

Let's do an example.

36. Why did Becky call?

(A) To ask to play baseball
(B) To invite Peter to her party
(C) To talk about a happy moment

The answer is "B." Fill in "B" on your answer sheet for question 36.

Now, you do it.

---

37. Why did David call?

(A) To take a test with Jill
(B) To ask about the answers
(C) To invite Jill to study together

38. Why did the father call?

(A) To decide the dinner menu
(B) To talk about the violin teacher
(C) To ask about the practice time

Go On

Listening

39. Why did the coach bring food?

(A) To eat it for lunch

(B) To celebrate the team's win

(C) To relax before practice

40. Why should the students see the school nurse?

(A) To take a nap

(B) To get some medicine

(C) To say they don't feel well

41. What does the teacher want Min-ho to do?

(A) Take more piano lessons

(B) Give the student his book

(C) Return the book to the library

You finished the listening test.

Memo

EXAMPLE

YES	NO	NO	NO	NO
A B ●	A B ✓	A B ✗	A B ▪	A B ⊘

Print your name in your first language:

Test Center Name:

Form Code:

Test Date:

SCHOOL USE ONLY
Is Consent Form on file? ◯ Yes ◯ No

1. NAME: Print your name. Using one box for each letter, first print your Given (first) name, then your Family (last) name
Below each box, use a No. 2 pencil and fill in the circle matching the same letter

GIVEN (FIRST) NAME | FAMILY (LAST) NAME

2. STUDENT NUMBER — Start here

3. DATE OF BIRTH
Month | Day | Year
Jan, Feb, Mar, Apr, May, Jun, Jul, Aug, Sep, Oct, Nov, Dec

4. GENDER
BOY ◯
GIRL ◯

5. COUNTRY CODE

6. LANGUAGE CODE

7. At my school, I am in:
◯ Grade 1
◯ Grade 2
◯ Grade 3
◯ Grade 4
◯ Grade 5
◯ Grade 6
◯ Grade 7
◯ Grade 8
◯ Grade 9
◯ Other

8. I have studied English for:
◯ 1 year or less
◯ 2 years
◯ 3 years
◯ 4 years
◯ 5 years
◯ 6 years or more

9. What test(s) have you taken before?
◯ TOEFL Primary Step 1
◯ TOEFL Primary Step 2
◯ Both
◯ None

10. GROUP CODE (If assigned)

11. CODE SETS (If assigned)
CODE SET 1 | CODE SET 2 | CODE SET 3

PAGE 1

Reading

1.	Ⓐ	Ⓑ	Ⓒ
2.	Ⓐ	Ⓑ	Ⓒ
3.	Ⓐ	Ⓑ	Ⓒ
4.	Ⓐ	Ⓑ	Ⓒ
5.	Ⓐ	Ⓑ	Ⓒ
6.	Ⓐ	Ⓑ	Ⓒ
7.	Ⓐ	Ⓑ	Ⓒ
8.	Ⓐ	Ⓑ	Ⓒ
9.	Ⓐ	Ⓑ	Ⓒ
10.	Ⓐ	Ⓑ	Ⓒ
11.	Ⓐ	Ⓑ	Ⓒ
12.	Ⓐ	Ⓑ	Ⓒ
13.	Ⓐ	Ⓑ	Ⓒ

14.	Ⓐ	Ⓑ	Ⓒ
15.	Ⓐ	Ⓑ	Ⓒ
16.	Ⓐ	Ⓑ	Ⓒ
17.	Ⓐ	Ⓑ	Ⓒ
18.	Ⓐ	Ⓑ	Ⓒ
19.	Ⓐ	Ⓑ	Ⓒ
20.	Ⓐ	Ⓑ	Ⓒ
21.	Ⓐ	Ⓑ	Ⓒ
22.	Ⓐ	Ⓑ	Ⓒ
23.	Ⓐ	Ⓑ	Ⓒ
24.	Ⓐ	Ⓑ	Ⓒ
25.	Ⓐ	Ⓑ	Ⓒ
26.	Ⓐ	Ⓑ	Ⓒ

27.	Ⓐ	Ⓑ	Ⓒ
28.	Ⓐ	Ⓑ	Ⓒ
29.	Ⓐ	Ⓑ	Ⓒ
30.	Ⓐ	Ⓑ	Ⓒ
31.	Ⓐ	Ⓑ	Ⓒ
32.	Ⓐ	Ⓑ	Ⓒ
33.	Ⓐ	Ⓑ	Ⓒ
34.	Ⓐ	Ⓑ	Ⓒ
35.	Ⓐ	Ⓑ	Ⓒ
36.	Ⓐ	Ⓑ	Ⓒ
37.	Ⓐ	Ⓑ	Ⓒ
38.	Ⓐ	Ⓑ	Ⓒ
39.	Ⓐ	Ⓑ	Ⓒ

Listening

1.	Ⓐ	Ⓑ	Ⓒ
2.	Ⓐ	Ⓑ	Ⓒ
3.	Ⓐ	Ⓑ	Ⓒ
4.	Ⓐ	Ⓑ	Ⓒ
5.	Ⓐ	Ⓑ	Ⓒ
6.	Ⓐ	Ⓑ	Ⓒ
7.	Ⓐ	Ⓑ	Ⓒ
8.	Ⓐ	Ⓑ	Ⓒ
9.	Ⓐ	Ⓑ	Ⓒ
10.	Ⓐ	Ⓑ	Ⓒ
11.	Ⓐ	Ⓑ	Ⓒ
12.	Ⓐ	Ⓑ	Ⓒ
13.	Ⓐ	Ⓑ	Ⓒ
14.	Ⓐ	Ⓑ	Ⓒ

15.	Ⓐ	Ⓑ	Ⓒ
16.	Ⓐ	Ⓑ	Ⓒ
17.	Ⓐ	Ⓑ	Ⓒ
18.	Ⓐ	Ⓑ	Ⓒ
19.	Ⓐ	Ⓑ	Ⓒ
20.	Ⓐ	Ⓑ	Ⓒ
21.	Ⓐ	Ⓑ	Ⓒ
22.	Ⓐ	Ⓑ	Ⓒ
23.	Ⓐ	Ⓑ	Ⓒ
24.	Ⓐ	Ⓑ	Ⓒ
25.	Ⓐ	Ⓑ	Ⓒ
26.	Ⓐ	Ⓑ	Ⓒ
27.	Ⓐ	Ⓑ	Ⓒ
28.	Ⓐ	Ⓑ	Ⓒ

29.	Ⓐ	Ⓑ	Ⓒ
30.	Ⓐ	Ⓑ	Ⓒ
31.	Ⓐ	Ⓑ	Ⓒ
32.	Ⓐ	Ⓑ	Ⓒ
33.	Ⓐ	Ⓑ	Ⓒ
34.	Ⓐ	Ⓑ	Ⓒ
35.	Ⓐ	Ⓑ	Ⓒ
36.	Ⓐ	Ⓑ	Ⓒ
37.	Ⓐ	Ⓑ	Ⓒ
38.	Ⓐ	Ⓑ	Ⓒ
39.	Ⓐ	Ⓑ	Ⓒ
40.	Ⓐ	Ⓑ	Ⓒ
41.	Ⓐ	Ⓑ	Ⓒ

EXAMPLE

YES	NO	NO	NO	NO
A B ●	A B ✓	A B ✗	A B 🔒	A B ◎

Print your name in your first language:

Test Center Name:

Form Code:

Test Date:

SCHOOL USE ONLY
Is Consent Form on file? ○ Yes ○ No

1. NAME: Print your name. Using one box for each letter, first print your Given (first) name, then your Family (last) name. Below each box, use a No. 2 pencil and fill in the circle matching the same letter.

GIVEN (FIRST) NAME   FAMILY (LAST) NAME

2. STUDENT NUMBER — Start here

3. DATE OF BIRTH

Month: Jan, Feb, Mar, Apr, May, Jun, Jul, Aug, Sep, Oct, Nov, Dec
Day
Year

4. GENDER
○ BOY
○ GIRL

5. COUNTRY CODE

6. LANGUAGE CODE

7. At my school, I am in:
○ Grade 1
○ Grade 2
○ Grade 3
○ Grade 4
○ Grade 5
○ Grade 6
○ Grade 7
○ Grade 8
○ Grade 9
○ Other

8. I have studied English for:
○ 1 year or less
○ 2 years
○ 3 years
○ 4 years
○ 5 years
○ 6 years or more

9. What test(s) have you taken before?
○ TOEFL Primary Step 1
○ TOEFL Primary Step 2
○ Both
○ None

10. GROUP CODE (If assigned)

11. CODE SETS (If assigned)
CODE SET 1
CODE SET 2
CODE SET 3

PAGE 1

Reading

#				#				#			
1.	Ⓐ	Ⓑ	Ⓒ	14.	Ⓐ	Ⓑ	Ⓒ	27.	Ⓐ	Ⓑ	Ⓒ
2.	Ⓐ	Ⓑ	Ⓒ	15.	Ⓐ	Ⓑ	Ⓒ	28.	Ⓐ	Ⓑ	Ⓒ
3.	Ⓐ	Ⓑ	Ⓒ	16.	Ⓐ	Ⓑ	Ⓒ	29.	Ⓐ	Ⓑ	Ⓒ
4.	Ⓐ	Ⓑ	Ⓒ	17.	Ⓐ	Ⓑ	Ⓒ	30.	Ⓐ	Ⓑ	Ⓒ
5.	Ⓐ	Ⓑ	Ⓒ	18.	Ⓐ	Ⓑ	Ⓒ	31.	Ⓐ	Ⓑ	Ⓒ
6.	Ⓐ	Ⓑ	Ⓒ	19.	Ⓐ	Ⓑ	Ⓒ	32.	Ⓐ	Ⓑ	Ⓒ
7.	Ⓐ	Ⓑ	Ⓒ	20.	Ⓐ	Ⓑ	Ⓒ	33.	Ⓐ	Ⓑ	Ⓒ
8.	Ⓐ	Ⓑ	Ⓒ	21.	Ⓐ	Ⓑ	Ⓒ	34.	Ⓐ	Ⓑ	Ⓒ
9.	Ⓐ	Ⓑ	Ⓒ	22.	Ⓐ	Ⓑ	Ⓒ	35.	Ⓐ	Ⓑ	Ⓒ
10.	Ⓐ	Ⓑ	Ⓒ	23.	Ⓐ	Ⓑ	Ⓒ	36.	Ⓐ	Ⓑ	Ⓒ
11.	Ⓐ	Ⓑ	Ⓒ	24.	Ⓐ	Ⓑ	Ⓒ	37.	Ⓐ	Ⓑ	Ⓒ
12.	Ⓐ	Ⓑ	Ⓒ	25.	Ⓐ	Ⓑ	Ⓒ	38.	Ⓐ	Ⓑ	Ⓒ
13.	Ⓐ	Ⓑ	Ⓒ	26.	Ⓐ	Ⓑ	Ⓒ	39.	Ⓐ	Ⓑ	Ⓒ

Listening

#				#				#			
1.	Ⓐ	Ⓑ	Ⓒ	15.	Ⓐ	Ⓑ	Ⓒ	29.	Ⓐ	Ⓑ	Ⓒ
2.	Ⓐ	Ⓑ	Ⓒ	16.	Ⓐ	Ⓑ	Ⓒ	30.	Ⓐ	Ⓑ	Ⓒ
3.	Ⓐ	Ⓑ	Ⓒ	17.	Ⓐ	Ⓑ	Ⓒ	31.	Ⓐ	Ⓑ	Ⓒ
4.	Ⓐ	Ⓑ	Ⓒ	18.	Ⓐ	Ⓑ	Ⓒ	32.	Ⓐ	Ⓑ	Ⓒ
5.	Ⓐ	Ⓑ	Ⓒ	19.	Ⓐ	Ⓑ	Ⓒ	33.	Ⓐ	Ⓑ	Ⓒ
6.	Ⓐ	Ⓑ	Ⓒ	20.	Ⓐ	Ⓑ	Ⓒ	34.	Ⓐ	Ⓑ	Ⓒ
7.	Ⓐ	Ⓑ	Ⓒ	21.	Ⓐ	Ⓑ	Ⓒ	35.	Ⓐ	Ⓑ	Ⓒ
8.	Ⓐ	Ⓑ	Ⓒ	22.	Ⓐ	Ⓑ	Ⓒ	36.	Ⓐ	Ⓑ	Ⓒ
9.	Ⓐ	Ⓑ	Ⓒ	23.	Ⓐ	Ⓑ	Ⓒ	37.	Ⓐ	Ⓑ	Ⓒ
10.	Ⓐ	Ⓑ	Ⓒ	24.	Ⓐ	Ⓑ	Ⓒ	38.	Ⓐ	Ⓑ	Ⓒ
11.	Ⓐ	Ⓑ	Ⓒ	25.	Ⓐ	Ⓑ	Ⓒ	39.	Ⓐ	Ⓑ	Ⓒ
12.	Ⓐ	Ⓑ	Ⓒ	26.	Ⓐ	Ⓑ	Ⓒ	40.	Ⓐ	Ⓑ	Ⓒ
13.	Ⓐ	Ⓑ	Ⓒ	27.	Ⓐ	Ⓑ	Ⓒ	41.	Ⓐ	Ⓑ	Ⓒ
14.	Ⓐ	Ⓑ	Ⓒ	28.	Ⓐ	Ⓑ	Ⓒ				

EXAMPLE

YES	NO	NO	NO	NO
Ⓐ ●	Ⓐ Ⓑ ✓	Ⓐ Ⓑ ✗	Ⓐ ▨ Ⓒ	Ⓐ Ⓑ ◎

Print your name in your first language:

Test Center Name:

Form Code:

Test Date:

SCHOOL USE ONLY
Is Consent Form on file? ○ Yes ○ No

1. NAME: Print your name. Using one box for each letter, first print your Given (first) name, then your Family (last) name. Below each box, use a No. 2 pencil and fill in the circle matching the same letter.

GIVEN (FIRST) NAME | **FAMILY (LAST) NAME**

2. STUDENT NUMBER — Start here

3. DATE OF BIRTH
Month | Day | Year

○ Jan
○ Feb
○ Mar
○ Apr
○ May
○ Jun
○ Jul
○ Aug
○ Sep
○ Oct
○ Nov
○ Dec

4. GENDER
BOY ○
GIRL ○

5. COUNTRY CODE

6. LANGUAGE CODE

7. At my school, I am in:
○ Grade 1
○ Grade 2
○ Grade 3
○ Grade 4
○ Grade 5
○ Grade 6
○ Grade 7
○ Grade 8
○ Grade 9
○ Other

8. I have studied English for:
○ 1 year or less
○ 2 years
○ 3 years
○ 4 years
○ 5 years
○ 6 years or more

9. What test(s) have you taken before?
○ TOEFL Primary Step 1
○ TOEFL Primary Step 2
○ Both
○ None

10. GROUP CODE (If assigned)

11. CODE SETS (If assigned)
CODE SET 1 | CODE SET 2 | CODE SET 3

PAGE 1

Reading

1. Ⓐ Ⓑ Ⓒ
2. Ⓐ Ⓑ Ⓒ
3. Ⓐ Ⓑ Ⓒ
4. Ⓐ Ⓑ Ⓒ
5. Ⓐ Ⓑ Ⓒ
6. Ⓐ Ⓑ Ⓒ
7. Ⓐ Ⓑ Ⓒ
8. Ⓐ Ⓑ Ⓒ
9. Ⓐ Ⓑ Ⓒ
10. Ⓐ Ⓑ Ⓒ
11. Ⓐ Ⓑ Ⓒ
12. Ⓐ Ⓑ Ⓒ
13. Ⓐ Ⓑ Ⓒ
14. Ⓐ Ⓑ Ⓒ
15. Ⓐ Ⓑ Ⓒ
16. Ⓐ Ⓑ Ⓒ
17. Ⓐ Ⓑ Ⓒ
18. Ⓐ Ⓑ Ⓒ
19. Ⓐ Ⓑ Ⓒ
20. Ⓐ Ⓑ Ⓒ
21. Ⓐ Ⓑ Ⓒ
22. Ⓐ Ⓑ Ⓒ
23. Ⓐ Ⓑ Ⓒ
24. Ⓐ Ⓑ Ⓒ
25. Ⓐ Ⓑ Ⓒ
26. Ⓐ Ⓑ Ⓒ
27. Ⓐ Ⓑ Ⓒ
28. Ⓐ Ⓑ Ⓒ
29. Ⓐ Ⓑ Ⓒ
30. Ⓐ Ⓑ Ⓒ
31. Ⓐ Ⓑ Ⓒ
32. Ⓐ Ⓑ Ⓒ
33. Ⓐ Ⓑ Ⓒ
34. Ⓐ Ⓑ Ⓒ
35. Ⓐ Ⓑ Ⓒ
36. Ⓐ Ⓑ Ⓒ
37. Ⓐ Ⓑ Ⓒ
38. Ⓐ Ⓑ Ⓒ
39. Ⓐ Ⓑ Ⓒ

Listening

1. Ⓐ Ⓑ Ⓒ
2. Ⓐ Ⓑ Ⓒ
3. Ⓐ Ⓑ Ⓒ
4. Ⓐ Ⓑ Ⓒ
5. Ⓐ Ⓑ Ⓒ
6. Ⓐ Ⓑ Ⓒ
7. Ⓐ Ⓑ Ⓒ
8. Ⓐ Ⓑ Ⓒ
9. Ⓐ Ⓑ Ⓒ
10. Ⓐ Ⓑ Ⓒ
11. Ⓐ Ⓑ Ⓒ
12. Ⓐ Ⓑ Ⓒ
13. Ⓐ Ⓑ Ⓒ
14. Ⓐ Ⓑ Ⓒ
15. Ⓐ Ⓑ Ⓒ
16. Ⓐ Ⓑ Ⓒ
17. Ⓐ Ⓑ Ⓒ
18. Ⓐ Ⓑ Ⓒ
19. Ⓐ Ⓑ Ⓒ
20. Ⓐ Ⓑ Ⓒ
21. Ⓐ Ⓑ Ⓒ
22. Ⓐ Ⓑ Ⓒ
23. Ⓐ Ⓑ Ⓒ
24. Ⓐ Ⓑ Ⓒ
25. Ⓐ Ⓑ Ⓒ
26. Ⓐ Ⓑ Ⓒ
27. Ⓐ Ⓑ Ⓒ
28. Ⓐ Ⓑ Ⓒ
29. Ⓐ Ⓑ Ⓒ
30. Ⓐ Ⓑ Ⓒ
31. Ⓐ Ⓑ Ⓒ
32. Ⓐ Ⓑ Ⓒ
33. Ⓐ Ⓑ Ⓒ
34. Ⓐ Ⓑ Ⓒ
35. Ⓐ Ⓑ Ⓒ
36. Ⓐ Ⓑ Ⓒ
37. Ⓐ Ⓑ Ⓒ
38. Ⓐ Ⓑ Ⓒ
39. Ⓐ Ⓑ Ⓒ
40. Ⓐ Ⓑ Ⓒ
41. Ⓐ Ⓑ Ⓒ

ワークブック

Step 1

Lesson 1 What is your name?

A Word List

新しい単語を読んで覚えましょう。

1	**monkey**	n	サル
2	**eraser**	n	消しゴム
3	**grape**	n	ブドウ
4	**blouse**	n	ブラウス
5	**shoulder**	n	肩（かた）
6	**toe**	n	足の指
7	**finger**	n	指
8	**mirror**	n	鏡
9	**clock**	n	時計
10	**watermelon**	n	スイカ
11	**strawberry**	n	イチゴ
12	**cap**	n	帽子（ぼうし）
13	**skirt**	n	スカート
14	**rabbit**	n	ウサギ
15	**ear**	n	耳

B Word Study

正しい単語を選びましょう。

1. I eat (grapes / blouses) and apples.

2. I have ten (ears / fingers).

3. She wears a (clock / skirt).

4. Do you have a (toe / mirror) in the bathroom?

5. I wear a(n) (cap / eraser) on a sunny day.

C Chunk Study

_____に正しい表現を書きましょう。

> from head to toe　　　　a pet rabbit　　　　a monkey in the tree
> wear a blouse　　　　on his shoulder

1. He put the bird _____.
   彼は鳥を肩の上に乗せた。

2. I want to have _____.
   私はペット用のウサギを飼いたい。

3. I want to _____ today.
   今日私はブラウスを着たい。

4. Bears are brown _____.
   クマは頭からつま先まで茶色だ。

5. There is _____.
   木の中にサルが1匹いる。

Lesson 2 How are you?

A Word List

新しい単語を読んで覚えましょう。

1	**smile**	v	笑う		
2	**shake**	v	振る		
3	**paint**	v	描く		
4	**stand**	v	立つ		
5	**warm**	adj	暖かい		
6	**cloudy**	adj	くもりの		
7	**fast**	adj	速い		
8	**help**	v	助ける		
9	**learn**	v	学ぶ		
10	**dark**	adj	暗い		
11	**drive**	v	運転する		
12	**walk**	v	歩く		
13	**jump**	v	ジャンプする		
14	**brown**	adj	茶色の		
15	**round**	adj	まるい		

B Word Study

正しい単語を選びましょう。

1. He (shakes / smiles) his hand.

2. Sarah likes to (stand / paint) a picture.

3. It is (warm / drive) today.

4. I (help / walk) to school every day.

5. The cats (jump / learn) on the table.

C Chunk Study

_____ に正しい表現を書きましょう。

> a round table　　　fast and easy　　　standing in line
> a big smile　　　dark brown

1. The boys are _____ .
   その男の子たちは列に並んでいる。

2. He entered with _____ .
   彼は大きな笑みを浮かべながら入ってきた。

3. There is _____ in the living room.
   居間にはまるいテーブルがある。

4. It is _____ .
   それは速くて簡単だ。

5. She has _____ eyes.
   彼女はこげ茶色の目をしている。

Lesson 3 What is she doing?

A Word List

新しい単語を読んで覚えましょう。

1	choose	v	選ぶ		
2	ring	v	鳴る		
3	sleep	v	眠る		
4	order	v	注文する		
5	wait	v	待つ		
6	ride	v	（乗り物に）乗る		
7	kick	v	ける		
8	catch	v	キャッチする		
9	fly	v	飛ぶ		
10	hold	v	持っている		
11	wear	v	着る		
12	cotton candy	n	綿あめ		
13	thirsty	adj	のどがかわいた		
14	bright	adj	明るい		
15	raise	v	（手を）あげる		

226

B Word Study

正しい単語を選びましょう。

1. This skirt is (thirsty / **bright**) yellow.

2. She (**kicks** / catches) the door open.

3. The alarm was (flying / **ringing**) at night.

4. He (**orders** / wears) a large pizza.

5. You can (wait / **choose**) many apples.

C Chunk Study

_____ に正しい表現を書きましょう。

> sleeping on the bed   wait for a while   ride a bicycle
> holding his hat   raise a hand

1. Please ___wait for a while___ .
   少し待ってください。

2. I like to ___ride a bicycle___ .
   私は自転車に乗るのが好きだ。

3. He is ___holding his hat___ in his hand.
   彼は手に帽子を持っている。

4. My cat is ___sleeping on the bed___ .
   私のネコはベッドの上で眠っている。

5. They didn't ___raise a hand___ .
   彼らは手をあげなかった。

Lesson 4 Which is bigger?

A Word List

新しい単語を読んで覚えましょう。

1	short	adj	背が低い, 短い
2	clean	adj	清潔な
3	same	adj	同じ
4	heavy	adj	重い
5	square	n	正方形
6	triangle	n	三角形
7	behind	prep	〜の後ろに
8	pool	n	水たまり
9	elephant	n	ゾウ
10	belt	n	ベルト
11	wide	adj	(幅が) 広い
12	happy	adj	幸福な
13	building	n	建物, ビル
14	high	adj	高い
15	coat	n	コート

B Word Study

正しい単語を選びましょう。

1. Wash your hands with (behind / clean) water.

2. He put a (belt / heavy) around his waist.

3. They are playing in the (pool / wide).

4. My cat's ears look like (squares / triangles).

5. Your (short / happy) smile is beautiful.

C Chunk Study

_____ に正しい表現を書きましょう。

> the same size　　　the highest score　　　a new building
> too short for you　　　heavy school bags

1. _____ can hurt your back.
   重いランドセルは背中を痛めることがある。

2. The skirt is _____ .
   そのスカートは君には短すぎる。

3. Our company bought _____ .
   私たちの会社は新しい建物を買った。

4. She got _____ in the test.
   彼女は試験で最高得点を取った。

5. This cup and that cup are _____ .
   このカップとあのカップは同じ大きさだ。

Lesson 5 What is it?

A Word List

新しい単語を読んで覚えましょう。

1	**squid**	n	イカ		
2	**farmer**	n	農夫		
3	**cherry**	n	サクランボ		
4	**badminton**	n	バドミントン		
5	**potato**	n	ジャガイモ		
6	**carrot**	n	ニンジン		
7	**bean**	n	豆		
8	**library**	n	図書館		
9	**holiday**	n	休日		
10	**alligator**	n	ワニ		
11	**corn**	n	トウモロコシ		
12	**pepper**	n	コショウ，トウガラシ		
13	**octopus**	n	タコ		
14	**starfish**	n	ヒトデ		
15	**lizard**	n	トカゲ		

B Word Study

正しい単語を選びましょう。

1. (A squid / A lizard) has ten soft arms.

2. They are playing (cherry / badminton) in the park.

3. Some (corns / peppers) are very hot.

4. (A starfish / An alligator) lives in the sea.

5. (Cherries / Beans) are small and round fruit.

C Chunk Study

_____に正しい表現を書きましょう。

> potato chips   bake a carrot cake   traditional holidays
> animals like an octopus   borrow books

1. _____ don't have a backbone.
   タコのような動物は背骨がない。

2. It is one of the biggest _____.
   それは最も盛大な伝統ある祝日の1つだ。

3. I bought _____.
   私はポテトチップスを買った。

4. Mom likes to _____.
   母はニンジンケーキを作るのが好きだ。

5. I usually _____ from the library.
   私はたいてい図書館で本を借りる。

Lesson 6 How does it look?

A Word List

新しい単語を読んで覚えましょう。

1	shout	v	叫ぶ		
2	slide	v	滑る		
3	introduce	v	紹介する		
4	whisper	v	ささやく		
5	march	v	行進する		
6	throw	v	投げる		
7	huge	adj	巨大な		
8	explain	v	説明する		
9	lead	v	率いる，導く		
10	carry	v	運ぶ		
11	colorful	adj	さまざまな色の		
12	blow	v	（口で）吹く		
13	swing	v	振る		
14	travel	v	旅行する		
15	scary	adj	怖い		

B Word Study

正しい単語を選びましょう。

1. The man looks (carry / scary), but he is kind.

2. Many people will (march / swing) in the parade.

3. The green leaves will be (blow / colorful) leaves in fall.

4. Let me (slide / introduce) our new team member.

5. You can (huge / throw) the ball to me.

C Chunk Study

_____に正しい表現を書きましょう。

| blow out | shouted with | lead the team |
| traveling around | | whispered into |

1. When we won the game, we _____ joy.
   私たちがその試合で勝った時，喜びの歓声をあげた。

2. He _____ my ear in the library.
   彼は図書館で私の耳にささやいた。

3. My dream is _____ the world.
   私の夢は世界を旅行することだ。

4. She will _____ next year.
   彼女は来年チームを率いることになる。

5. Let's _____ the candles together.
   ろうそくをいっしょに吹き消しましょう。

Lesson 7: When is the event?

A Word List

新しい単語を読んで覚えましょう。

1	space	n	宇宙（うちゅう）		
2	favorite	adj	一番好きな		
3	subject	n	科目		
4	gym	n	体育，体育館		
5	vegetable	n	野菜		
6	fruit	n	果物		
7	fried rice	n	チャーハン		
8	beef	n	牛肉		
9	arrive	v	到着（とうちゃく）する		
10	recess	n	休み時間		
11	invite	v	招待する		
12	yearly	adj	毎年ある		
13	relay race	n	リレー競走		
14	jump rope	n	なわとび		
15	participate	v	参加する		

B Word Study

正しい単語を選びましょう。

1. Many people want to travel into (yearly / space).

2. (Beef / Fruit) comes from cows.

3. I (participated / invited) my friends to my birthday party.

4. You should eat more (vegetables / fried rice) such as carrots.

5. It is a (gym / relay race) between the two teams.

C Chunk Study

_____に正しい表現を書きましょう。

> do jump rope　　　favorite subject　　　during recess
> in gym class　　　arrive at

1. My _____ is music.
   私が一番好きな科目は音楽だ。

2. He will _____ the station.
   彼は駅に到着する予定だ。

3. Students play in the playground _____.
   生徒たちは休み時間に運動場で遊ぶ。

4. My plan is to _____ every day.
   私の計画は毎日なわとびをすることだ。

5. The kids are learning fun activities _____.
   子どもたちが体育の時間に楽しい運動を学んでいる。

Lesson 8 What is the letter about?

A Word List

新しい単語を読んで覚えましょう。

1	useful	adj	有用な		
2	object	n	物体		
3	return	v	返ってくる		
4	vacation	n	休暇（きゅうか）		
5	enjoy	v	楽しむ		
6	forget	v	忘（わす）れる		
7	penguin	n	ペンギン		
8	skateboard	n	スケートボード		
9	board	n	板		
10	stripe	n	しま模様（もよう）		
11	can't wait to		早く〜したい		
12	get rest		休息する		
13	throw into the air		空中に投げる		
14	start a fire		火をおこす		
15	spin in a circle		円を描（えが）いて回る		

B Word Study

正しい単語を選びましょう。

1. I got a lot of (object / **useful**) information from books.

2. Where did you go during your summer (**vacation** / stripe)?

3. Did you (penguin / **forget**) to bring your book?

4. He likes to ride a (enjoy / **skateboard**) in the park.

5. They stand at each end of a long (**board** / return).

C Chunk Study

_____に正しい表現を書きましょう。

> get some rest　　　spin in a circle　　　start a fire
> can't wait to　　　threw the ball into

1. People used dry wood to _____ at night.
   人々は夜に火をおこすために乾いた木を使った。

2. You look tired. You need to _____ .
   あなたは疲れているようです。少し休んだほうがよいですよ。

3. I _____ see my classmates again.
   私はクラスの友達と早くまた会いたい。

4. My dog liked to _____ .
   私の犬は円を描いてくるくる回るのが好きだった。

5. She _____ the air.
   彼女は空中にボールを投げた。

Lesson 9: What is on the desk?

A Word List

新しい単語を読んで覚えましょう。

1	candle	n	ろうそく
2	pet	v	なだめる，なでる，かわいがる
3	small	adj	小さい，少ない
4	sweater	n	セーター
5	television	n	テレビ
6	hurt	v	傷つける，傷める
7	knee	n	ひざ
8	singing contest	n	歌唱大会
9	scared	adj	怖がって
10	snake	n	ヘビ
11	a pair of		一組の
12	look at		〜を見る
13	next to		〜のすぐ横に
14	instead of		〜の代わりに
15	win first place		優勝する

B Word Study

正しい単語を選びましょう。

1. I saw a (snake / shout) in my backyard.

2. The blue (elephant / sweater) is small for you.

3. How many (seats / candles) do you need for your cake?

4. Many children like to (pet / wear) dogs.

5. She is (warm / scared) to stay home alone.

C Chunk Study

_____ に正しい表現を書きましょう。

| look at | win first place | next to me |
| instead of | | a pair of shoes |

1. You can put water _____ milk in your hot chocolate.
   ココアには牛乳の代わりにお湯を入れてもいい。

2. When did she _____ at the Olympics?
   いつ彼女はオリンピックで優勝しましたか？

3. I paid $50 for _____ .
   私は靴一足に50ドルを支払った。

4. _____ the camera and smile.
   カメラを見てほほえんでください。

5. Why don't you sit _____ ?
   私のとなりに座ったらどうですか？

Lesson 10 — What did she say?

A Word List

新しい単語を読んで覚えましょう。

1	**wild animal**	n	野生動物
2	**lap**	n	ひざ，ももの上
3	**toothpaste**	n	練り歯磨き
4	**toothbrush**	n	歯ブラシ
5	**hallway**	n	廊下
6	**bump**	v	ぶつかる
7	**memorize**	v	暗記する
8	**meaning**	n	意味
9	**front**	n	前，前面
10	**back**	n	後ろ，背面
11	**go for a walk**		散歩する
12	**put on**		～をはく，～を着る
13	**come over**		やって来る，立ち寄る
14	**take a long time**		長く時間がかかる
15	**calm down**		落ち着く，気をしずめる

B Word Study

正しい単語を選びましょう。

1. How did you (bump / memorize) all the songs in the show?

2. I saw my dad's car in (front / board) of my school.

3. Do not run in the (hallway / subject).

4. What is the (color / meaning) of the sentence?

5. How often should I change my (toothbrush / lap)?

C Chunk Study

_____に正しい表現を書きましょう。

| calm down | put on | come over to my house |
| go for a walk | | take a long time |

1. It will _____ to forget you.
   君を忘れるには長い時間がかかるだろう。

2. You need to _____ after a big fight with your friend.
   友達と大いにけんかした後には落ち着く必要があります。

3. Will you _____ this afternoon?
   今日の午後に私の家に寄ってくれませんか？

4. My parents like to _____ after dinner.
   私の両親は夕食の後に散歩に行くのが好きだ。

5. It's cold outside. _____ your jacket.
   外は寒いです。上着を着なさい。

Lesson 11 Can you help me?

A Word List

新しい単語を読んで覚えましょう。

1	**soon**	adv	すぐに		
2	**race**	n	競走，試合		
3	**trip**	v	つまずく		
4	**scare**	v	怖がらせる，驚かす		
5	**locker**	n	ロッカー		
6	**right-handed**	adj	右ききの		
7	**forward**	adv	前に		
8	**seat**	n	席		
9	**full**	adj	いっぱいの		
10	**decide**	v	決定する		
11	**be good at**		～が得意だ，～が上手だ		
12	**fall down**		転ぶ		
13	**on the left**		左に		
14	**sit down**		座る		
15	**right now**		今すぐ		

B Word Study

正しい単語を選びましょう。

1. The bakery is (huge / full) of cakes and bread.

2. Did you (decide / help) what to wear to the party?

3. Walk (soon / forward) until you see a building.

4. Can you keep my books in your (locker / skateboard)?

5. Be careful you don't (trip / catch) over the mat.

C Chunk Study

_____に正しい表現を書きましょう。

> right now   are good at   sit down
> on the left   fell down the stairs

1. What subject _____ you _____?
   君はどの科目が得意なの？

2. Turn right and the restaurant is _____.
   右に曲がるとそのレストランが左側にあります。

3. Please come in and _____.
   中に入ってお座りください。

4. Should I call him _____?
   私が彼に今すぐ電話しましょうか？

5. I _____ yesterday.
   私は昨日階段で転んだ。

Lesson 12 How are you feeling?

A Word List

新しい単語を読んで覚えましょう。

1	**job**	n	仕事，課題
2	**remember**	v	覚えている，思い出す
3	**water**	v	水をやる
4	**dessert**	n	デザート
5	**flavor**	n	（独特な）味
6	**discount**	n	値引き
7	**perfect**	adj	完全な，完ぺきな
8	**zipper**	n	ジッパー，ファスナー
9	**pants**	n	ズボン
10	**agree**	v	同意する
11	**in a few days**		2，3日で
12	**be worried**		心配する
13	**a sale on**		〜のセール
14	**on the radio**		ラジオで
15	**look like**		〜のように見える

B Word Study

正しい単語を選びましょう。

1. What (flavor / corn) of candy do you like?

2. It's a (wide / perfect) day for a picnic.

3. My mom told me to (water / fly) the plants.

4. The (belt / zipper) on my jacket is stuck.

5. I'm buying ten pairs of shoes. Could you give me a (discount / break)?

C Chunk Study

_____ に正しい表現を書きましょう。

> look like a princess   a sale on toys   on the radio
> is worried about   in a few days

1. I heard the news _____ .
   私はラジオでそのニュースを聞いた。

2. My teacher _____ my grades.
   先生は私の成績について心配している。

3. They are having _____ until this weekend.
   今週末までおもちゃのセールがあります。

4. You _____ in that dress.
   君がそのドレスを着るとお姫様みたいに見えるよ。

5. I'll call you _____ .
   数日中に電話しますよ。

Lesson 13 What does he want?

A Word List

新しい単語を読んで覚えましょう。

1	clay	n	土, 粘土（ねんど）		
2	track	n	（競走の）トラック		
3	switch	v	換（か）える, 転換（てんかん）する		
4	tie	v	ひもで結ぶ		
5	review	n	復習		
6	headache	n	頭痛（ずつう）		
7	knock	v	たたく, 割（わ）る		
8	ladder	n	はしご		
9	remind	v	再度知らせる		
10	stack	v	積む, 重ねる		
11	hang up		（絵や服を）掛（か）ける, つるす		
12	turn out		～だと明らかになる		
13	get it		理解する		
14	as soon as possible		できるだけ早く		
15	put away		（物を）片（かた）づける		

B Word Study

正しい単語を選びましょう。

1. Can you (remind / memorize) me to buy an eraser?

2. He will need a (hallway / ladder) to get onto the roof.

3. I usually (tie / lead) my hair when it's hot.

4. Don't (stand / stack) books on the table.

5. We learned how to make a (flavor / clay) cup at school.

C Chunk Study

_____に正しい表現を書きましょう。

> get it　　　hang up your coat　　　turned out to be
> put away your toys　　　as soon as possible

1. It's time to _____ and go to bed.
   おもちゃを片づけてベッドに入る時間ですよ。

2. Please come see me _____ .
   できるだけ早く私に会いに来てください。

3. _____ and sit down in your chair.
   コートを掛けていすに座りなさい。

4. I don't _____ _____ . Can you explain it more?
   よくわかりません。それについてもっと説明してもらえますか。

5. His friend _____ a liar.
   彼の友達はうそつきであることが明らかになった。

Lesson 14 What will she do next?

A Word List

新しい単語を読んで覚えましょう。

1	smooth	adj	なめらかな, やわらかい		
2	scoop	n	（アイスクリームの）スクープ, ひとすくい		
3	napkin	n	ナプキン		
4	right	n	右側		
5	boring	adj	退屈な		
6	believe	v	信じる		
7	awesome	adj	すごい, かっこいい		
8	advice	n	助言, 忠告		
9	watch	n	腕時計		
10	serving	n	（食べ物の）一人前		
11	how come ~?		なぜ, どうして（～なのか）？		
12	a couple of		2つの		
13	run out of		～がなくなる		
14	too far from		～からとても遠い		
15	by chance		偶然に, 意外にも		

B Word Study

正しい単語を選びましょう。

1. How many (races / scoops) of ice cream do you want?

2. This recipe is for four (candles / servings).

3. The school has a(n) (awesome / cloudy) art teacher.

4. My father is a (full / smooth) driver.

5. We should listen to the teacher's (advice / cap).

C Chunk Study

_____に正しい表現を書きましょう。

| by chance | how come | a couple of notebooks |
| too far from | running out of gas | |

1. Bring _____ .
   ノートを2冊持ってきなさい。

2. The supermarket is _____ my house.
   スーパーマーケットは私の家からとても遠い。

3. I met my teacher in my neighborhood _____ .
   偶然に近所で先生と会った。

4. _____ you didn't come to school today?
   どうして今日は学校に来なかったの？

5. His car is _____ .
   彼の車はガソリンが切れかかっている。

Lesson 15 Why did he call?

A Word List

新しい単語を読んで覚えましょう。

1	guest	n	客		
2	sign	v	署名する		
3	pour	v	注ぐ		
4	coach	n	（スポーツチームの）コーチ		
5	mean	adj	嫌な，意地の悪い		
6	permission	n	許可		
7	tired	adj	疲れた		
8	different	adj	他の		
9	safe	adj	安全な		
10	keep	v	持っている，保管する		
11	remember to		忘れずに～する		
12	lots of		多くの		
13	by the way		ところで		
14	look around		見回す		
15	get to		～に到着する		

B Word Study

正しい単語を選びましょう。

1. Can you (tie / **pour**) me some water?

2. If you feel (**tired** / useful), get some sleep.

3. We have a (**guest** / front) at our house tonight.

4. Please (pet / **sign**) your name here.

5. My sister and I look (favorite / **different**).

C Chunk Study

_____に正しい表現を書きましょう。

| lots of people | get to | by the way |
| look around the museum | | remember to mail |

1. You must call your mom when you _____ your friend's house.
   友達の家に着いたらお母さんに電話しなければならない。

2. There are _____ in the movie theater.
   映画館にたくさんの人たちがいる。

3. Why are you here, _____?
   ところで君はどうしてここにいるの？

4. _____ this letter.
   忘れずにこの手紙を出しなさい。

5. You have one hour to _____.
   あなたたちが博物館を見て回る時間は1時間です。

Lesson 16 What is he talking about?

A Word List

新しい単語を読んで覚えましょう。

1	book fair	n	図書展示会（てんじかい）		
2	runner	n	走者		
3	medal	n	メダル		
4	ankle	n	足首		
5	costume	n	衣装（いしょう）		
6	fake	adj	にせの，模造（もぞう）の		
7	blood	n	血，血液		
8	extra	adv	特別に		
9	soap	n	石けん		
10	cough	v	せきをする		
11	take a photo		写真を撮（と）る		
12	write down		記入する		
13	share with		〜と分け合う		
14	for example		たとえば		
15	get a cold		かぜをひく		

B Word Study

正しい単語を選びましょう。

1. She often hurts her (headache / **ankle**).

2. What (**costume** / meaning) should I wear on Halloween?

3. My brother found (short / **fake**) money on the street.

4. Cover your mouth when you (**cough** / tie).

5. Who is the fastest (job / **runner**) on your team?

C Chunk Study

_____に正しい表現を書きましょう。

> get a cold　　　　for example　　　　take a photo
> write down your name　　　　share with her classmates

1. I'd like to _____ with my art teacher.
   私は美術の先生といっしょに写真を撮りたいと思う。

2. If you play outside for too long, you may _____.
   あまり長く外で遊べばかぜをひいてしまうかもしれない。

3. There are many school events. _____, there are sports day and movie night.
   学校の行事は多い。たとえば運動会や，映画の上映会がある。

4. Please _____, phone number and address.
   名前，電話番号と住所を記入してください。

5. She brought some cookies to _____.
   彼女はクラスの友達と分け合って食べるためのクッキーを持ってきた。

Memo

Memo

●TOEFL Primary®についての情報は、こちらにお問い合わせください。
株式会社公文教育研究会　アセスメント事業推進部
E-mail:toefl_info@kumon.co.jp
https://gc-t.jp

監修●株式会社公文教育研究会　アセスメント事業推進部
装丁●タカハシデザイン室
表紙イラストレーション●木下綾乃

はじめての TOEFL Primary® テスト問題集 Step 1

2015年 3月13日　初版第 1 刷発行
2025年 2月 3日　初版第10刷発行

発行人●泉田義則
発行所●株式会社くもん出版
〒141-8488　東京都品川区東五反田2-10-2 東五反田スクエア11F
編集　　03-6836-0317
営業　　03-6836-0305
代表　　03-6836-0301

印刷・製本●TOPPANクロレ株式会社

©2015 KUMON PUBLISHING Co.,LTD　Printed in Japan
ISBN 978-4-7743-2387-9

落丁・乱丁本はおとりかえします。
本書を無断で複写・複製・転載・翻訳することは、法律で認められた場合を除き禁じられています。
購入者以外の第三者による本書のいかなる電子複製も一切認められていませんのでご注意ください。
CD58844

Preparation Book for the TOEFL Primary Step 1
Copyright © 2014 by Ji Taek Lim
All rights reserved.
Original Korean edition published in Korea in 2014 by Metacurio Inc.
Japanese translation rights arranged with Metacurio Inc.
through Shinwon Agency Co. and Japan Foreign-Rights Centre

ETS, the ETS logo, トフル, TOEFL, TOEFL Junior and TOEFL Primary are registered trademarks of Educational Testing Service, Princeton, New Jersey, U.S.A., used in Japan under license by Kumon Institute of Education Co., Ltd.

くもん出版ホームページアドレス
https://kumonshuppan.com/

はじめての
TOEFL Primary® テスト問題集

監修●Global Communication & Testing

Step 1

解答・解説

くもん出版

はじめての
TOEFL Primary®
テスト
問題集

監修●Global Communication & Testing

Step 1

解答・解説

くもん出版

Lesson 1

■ 重要ポイント

確認問題
apple, pen, monkey, Anne, mountain, hospital

■ 練習問題

| 1. (A) | 2. (A) | 3. (B) | 4. (B) |
| 5. (A) | 6. (C) | 7. (B) | 8. (C) |

1. (A) サル
   (B) ライオン
   (C) トラ

2. (A) はさみ
   (B) マーカー（ペン）
   (C) 机

3. (A) ソファー
   (B) バスタブ
   (C) ベッド

4. (A) 机
   (B) 消しゴム
   (C) 時計

5. (A) 腕
   (B) 脚
   (C) 顔

6. (A) ブドウ
   (B) バナナ
   (C) モモ

7. (A) 手袋
   (B) シャツ
   (C) ブラウス

8. (A) 肩
   (B) 背中
   (C) 首

■ ミニテスト

| 1. (A) | 2. (C) | 3. (C) | 4. (B) |
| 5. (C) | 6. (B) | 7. (A) | 8. (C) |

1. (A) 足の指
   (B) 脚
   (C) 手の指

2. (A) クローゼット
   (B) ドア
   (C) 鏡

3. (A) 黒板
   (B) 本
   (C) 時計

4. (A) スイカ
   (B) イチゴ
   (C) レモン

5. (A) 帽子
   (B) ジーンズ（ジーパン）
   (C) スカート

6. (A) 牛
   (B) ウサギ
   (C) ブタ

7. (A) ブーツ
   (B) 運動靴
   (C) 手袋

8. (A) 口
   (B) 目
   (C) 耳

Lesson 2

■ 重要ポイント

確認問題
| 1. V | 2. A | 3. V | 4. A |
| 5. A | 6. V | 7. V | 8. A |

■ 練習問題

| 1. (B) | 2. (A) | 3. (B) | 4. (C) |
| 5. (B) | 6. (A) | 7. (C) | 8. (B) |

1. (A) 話す
   (B) 泣く
   (C) 笑う

2. (A) 歌う
   (B) 学ぶ
   (C) 振る

3. (A) 走る
   (B) 絵を描く
   (C) 字を書く

4. (A) 立ち止まる
   (B) 立つ
   (C) 座る

5. (A) 小さな本
   (B) 大きな本
   (C) 古い本

6. (A) 冷たい水
   (B) 温かい水
   (C) 熱い水（湯）

7. (A) 雪が降っている
   (B) くもっている
   (C) 雨が降っている

8. (A) 弱い
   (B) 強い
   (C) 長い

■ ミニテスト

| 1. (B) | 2. (A) | 3. (A) | 4. (B) |
| 5. (A) | 6. (C) | 7. (B) | 8. (C) |

1. (A) 出発する
   (B) 立つ
   (C) 立ち止まる

2. (A) 速い自動車
   (B) 速い列車
   (C) 大きな飛行機

3. (A) 食べる
   (B) 助ける
   (C) 学ぶ

4. (A) 日当たりがよい
   (B) 暗い
   (C) 明るい

5. (A) 運転する
   (B) 作る
   (C) 歩く

6. (A) あげる
   (B) 取る
   (C) ジャンプする

7. (A) やせたクマ
   (B) 太ったクマ
   (C) 弱いクマ

8. (A) 紫色の箱
   (B) まるい箱
   (C) 茶色の箱

Lesson 3

■ 重要ポイント

確認問題
1. I watch TV.
2. I walked to school.
3. I am talking to mom.

■ 練習問題

| 1. (C) | 2. (B) | 3. (B) | 4. (A) |
| 5. (C) | 6. (B) | 7. (C) | 8. (A) |

1. (A) 彼はバナナを選んでいる。
   (B) 彼女はリンゴを食べている。
   (C) 彼女はリンゴを選んでいる。

2. (A) 女の子は犬と泳いでいる。
   (B) 犬は女の子と走っている。
   (C) 女の子は犬と話をしている。

3. (A) 電話が寝室で鳴っている。
   (B) 目覚まし時計が寝室で鳴っている。
   (C) 目覚まし時計が居間で鳴っている。

4. (A) 男の子と女の子が本を読んでいる。
   (B) 男の子は女の子と歌を歌っている。
   (C) 女の子は本を読み，男の子は歌を歌う。

5. (A) ネコがソファーの上を歩いている。
   (B) ネコがクッションの下で寝ている。
   (C) ネコがクッションの上で寝ている。

6. (A) 男の人が本を読んでいる。
   (B) 男の人が食べ物を注文している。
   (C) 女の人がケーキをほしがっている。

7. (A) 彼女はバスを待っている。
   (B) 彼はバスに乗っている。
   (C) 彼はバスを待っている。

8. (A) 女の子がドラムをたたく。
   (B) 女の子がキーボードを弾いている。
   (C) ドラムは8つある。

■ ミニテスト

| 1. (C) | 2. (A) | 3. (B) | 4. (A) |
| 5. (A) | 6. (A) | 7. (C) | 8. (B) |

1. (A) 彼女は青いセーターを着ている。
   (B) 彼女は通りを走っている。
   (C) 彼女はインラインスケートで滑っている。

2. (A) 彼女はボールをけっている。
   (B) 彼らはボールで遊んでいる。
   (C) 彼女はボールをキャッチする。

3. (A) 彼らはおなかが空いていない。
   (B) 2羽の鳥が巣にいる。
   (C) 2羽の鳥が飛んでいる。

4. (A) キリンの首は長い。
   (B) 脚が3本ある。
   (C) キリンが走っている。

5. (A) 男の子はポップコーンを持っている。
   (B) 男の子は黄色いシャツを着ている。
   (C) 男の子は綿あめが嫌いだ。

6. (A) 彼は水を飲みたがっている。
   (B) 彼は寒がっている。
   (C) 彼はのどがかわいていない。

7. (A) 昨日はよく晴れた明るい天気だった。
   (B) 木がたくさんある。
   (C) 風がとても強い天気だ。

8. (A) 2冊の本が机の下にある。
   (B) その女の子は手を高くあげている。
   (C) その女の子は机の上に座っている。

Lesson 4

■ 重要ポイント

確認問題
1. faster
2. as rich as
3. the smartest
4. as tall as

■ 練習問題

| 1. (C) | 2. (B) | 3. (A) | 4. (B) |
| 5. (B) | 6. (C) | 7. (B) | 8. (A) |

1. (A) 3本の鉛筆が机の上にある。
   (B) 赤い鉛筆が一番長い。
   (C) 緑色の鉛筆は黄色い鉛筆より長い。

2. (A) ピンクのシャツは緑色のシャツよりも大きい。
   (B) ピンクのシャツは緑色のシャツと同じ大きさだ。
   (C) ピンクのシャツは緑色のシャツより小さい。

3. (A) 青いズボンをはいている女の子は，男の子と同じくらいの背の高さである。
   (B) 男の子がこのグループで一番背が高い。
   (C) 黄色いスカートをはいた女の子が一番背が低い。

4. (A) 茶色の手袋は青い手袋より大きい。
   (B) 青い手袋は茶色い手袋よりきれいだ。
   (C) 手袋の色は同じだ。

5. (A) ネズミはこのグループで一番重い動物である。
   (B) パンダはネズミより重い。
   (C) 絵の中に3匹のサルがいる。

6. (A) 紫色の三角形とオレンジ色の正方形は同じ大きさだ。
   (B) 緑色の円は紫色の三角形の横にある。
   (C) 三角形が一番大きい形だ。

7. (A) 家族の中でお父さんが一番背が高い。
   (B) 家族の中で赤ちゃんが一番年下だ。
   (C) 男の子はお母さんの横に立っている。

8. (A) その家は木の前にある。
   (B) その木は家の横にある。
   (C) その家は木の後ろにある。

■ ミニテスト

1. (B)	2. (C)	3. (A)	4. (B)
5. (A)	6. (B)	7. (B)	8. (C)

1. (A) 2匹のブタが水たまりで遊んでいる。
   (B) ゾウはブタより大きい。
   (C) ブタとゾウは同じ大きさだ。

2. (A) 黒いペンキの缶は黄色いペンキの缶よりも大きい。
   (B) 2つとも同じ色だ。
   (C) 黄色いペンキの缶は黒いペンキの缶と同じ大きさだ。

3. (A) 男の子は女の子より若い。
   (B) 女の子は男の子より小さい。
   (C) 2人ともとても年をとっている。

4. (A) どちらのベルトも同じ色だ。
   (B) 黄色いベルトは青いベルトよりも幅が広い。
   (C) 青いベルトは黄色いベルトと同じ幅の広さだ。

5. (A) 女の子は男の子より幸せだ。
   (B) 男の子と女の子は幸せだ。
   (C) 男の子は女の子より幸せだ。

6. (A) 緑色のビルは青いビルより高い。
   (B) オレンジ色のビルが一番高いビルだ。
   (C) 青いビルはオレンジ色のビルと同じ高さだ。

7. (A) テーブルの上にコートが2着ある。
   (B) コートはブラウスより暖かい。
   (C) ブラウスはコートより暖かい。

8. (A) 昨日は雨だった。
   (B) 昨日は今日よりも寒かった。
   (C) 今日は昨日より寒い。

Lesson 5

■ 重要ポイント

確認問題

1. a	2. an	3. x	4. x	5. a
6. an	7. a	8. x	9. x	

■ 練習問題

1. (B)	2. (B)	3. (A)	4. (C)
5. (A)	6. (A)	7. (B)	8. (A)

1. それは海で泳いでいます。それはするどい歯とヒレを持っています。それは＿＿＿＿です。
   (A) カエル
   (B) サメ
   (C) イカ

2. その人たちは農場で働いています。その人たちはあなたたちのために野菜を育てます。その人たちは力が強いです。その人たちは，だれですか？
   (A) 看護師
   (B) 農家の人
   (C) 牛

3. その人たちは映画に出ます。テレビにも出ます。その人たちを見てあなたは笑ったり泣いたりします。その人たちはだれですか？
   (A) 俳優
   (B) コック
   (C) 先生

4. それは甘いものです。それはふつう茶色です。こげ茶色のものもあれば，うす茶色のものもあります。それは何ですか？
   (A) サクランボ
   (B) オレンジ
   (C) チョコレート

5. あなたはこの運動をします。あなたはラケットを使います。あなたは黄色いボールを打ちます。それは何ですか？
   (A) テニス
   (B) 野球
   (C) バドミントン

6. それはサンドイッチの一種です。あなたはその上に肉とチーズを見つけることができます。それは何ですか？
   (A) ハンバーガー
   (B) パスタ
   (C) クッキー

7. これは健康によい食べ物です。これは野菜です。その色はオレンジ色です。それは何ですか？

(A) ジャガイモ
(B) ニンジン
(C) リンゴ

8. それはまるいものです。赤いもの、茶色いもの、黒いものがあります。それは食べ物です。それは何ですか？

(A) 豆
(B) ボール
(C) スイカ

■ ミニテスト

| 1. (C) | 2. (A) | 3. (C) | 4. (B) |
| 5. (A) | 6. (C) | 7. (B) | 8. (A) |

1. あなたはここで本を読むことができます。あなたはここで勉強もします。あなたはとても静かにしていなければなりません。そこはどこですか？

(A) 居間(いま)
(B) 店
(C) 図書館

2. この日には年をとります。パーティーをすることもあります。あなたの友達みんなが来ます。その日は何ですか？

(A) 誕生日(たんじょうび)
(B) 休日
(C) 会議

3. それは動物です。それは海辺に生息しています。それはまるい体をしていて、横向きに歩きます。それは何ですか？

(A) ワニ
(B) サメ
(C) カニ

4. それは黄色い色をしています。それには、たくさんの小さな実がなっています。あなたはそれをはじけるまでいっておやつにすることがあります。それを棒(ぼう)にさして食べることもあります。それは何ですか？

(A) 米
(B) トウモロコシ
(C) バナナ

5. それは緑色か、黄色か、または赤い色をしています。とても辛いこともあります。それは＿＿＿です。

(A) トウガラシ
(B) ブドウ
(C) タマネギ

6. あなたはそれを食べます。それはふつうまるくて甘(あま)いものです。チョコレートチップが入っているものもあります。それは何ですか？

(A) キャラメル
(B) ケーキ
(C) クッキー

7. それは海の生き物です。それは平べったく、5本の足があります。それは何ですか？

(A) タコ
(B) ヒトデ
(C) トカゲ

8. あなたはお金を受け取るためにここに行きます。また、あなたはここにお金を預けます。それは場所です。それは何ですか？

(A) 銀行
(B) スーパーマーケット
(C) 郵便局(ゆうびんきょく)

Lesson 6

■ 重要ポイント

確認問題
1. happy　　　2. hot　　　3. tall

■ 練習問題

1. (A)	2. (B)	3. (A)	4. (C)
5. (B)	6. (C)	7. (B)	8. (B)

1. それは先生が質問したときに，生徒たちがすることです。それは人々があなたの名前を呼んだときに，あなたがすることです。あなたは何をしますか？

   (A) 答える
   (B) ジャンプする
   (C) 叫ぶ

2. 雨がすることです。ガラスがこれをすると，ガラスは割れてしまいます。木は秋になると葉っぱをこのようにします。

   (A) 過ぎ去る
   (B) 落とす
   (C) 滑る

3. あなたが人と会うとまずしなければならないことです。人は発表を始めるときにもこれをします。もしあなたがこれをしなければ，他の人たちはあなたがだれなのかわかりません。あなたは何をしますか？

   (A) 紹介する
   (B) 閉める
   (C) 歌う

4. 人々が静かに話すとき，これをします。もしあなたが図書館にいるなら，こうしなければなりません。人々がこれをするとき，きちんと聞き取ることが難しいこともあります。人々は何をしますか？

   (A) 持ち上げる
   (B) 聞く
   (C) ささやく

5. 人々はこれを軍隊でします。また人々はパレードでこれをします。人々が集まって，いっしょに歩きます。人々は何をしますか？

   (A) 遊ぶ
   (B) 行進する
   (C) 運転する

6. あなたがある物に対してこれをすると，物は空中を飛んでゆきます。人は，野球の試合でこれをします。人がこれをすると，他のだれかがキャッチします。それは何ですか？

   (A) 傷つける
   (B) 走る
   (C) 投げる

7. もしだれかがこのような状態であれば，その人は健康ではないか，十分な筋肉を持っていません。その人は速く動くことができず，重い物を運ぶことができません。その人は＿＿＿＿です。

   (A) 強い
   (B) 弱い
   (C) かしこい

8. あなたが帽子をかぶり，手袋をはめたときにこのように感じることができます。太陽に当たったときも同じように感じます。これは熱を持っていますが，暑いと感じるほどではありません。それは何ですか？

   (A) 固い
   (B) 暖かい
   (C) 冷たい，寒い

■ ミニテスト

1. (B)	2. (B)	3. (A)	4. (A)
5. (A)	6. (C)	7. (C)	8. (C)

1. このような部屋は嫌われます。みなさんはこのような部屋を掃除しなければなりません。このような部屋はみなさんのお母さんを怒らせることでしょう。その部屋は＿＿＿＿です。

   (A) 小さい
   (B) きたない
   (C) 大きい

2. だれかがあなたに向かって何かを投げた後に，あなたはこれをします。野球用のグローブをつけてすることもあります。あなたは手を使ってその物を止めて捕まえます。あなたは何をしますか？

   (A) 説明する
   (B) キャッチする
   (C) 泣く

3. あなたがこれをすると，他の人はあなたの後について来ます。みんなに行き先を告げるときも，あなたはこれをします。また，あなたが（チームの）キャプテンならこれをします。それは何ですか？

   (A) 導く
   (B) 送る
   (C) 生きる

4. みなさんはかばんを持っているときに，これをします。赤ちゃんは歩けないので，これをしてもらわなければなりません。みなさんはまた友達が何かを持っているとき，助け

るためにこれをします。それは何ですか？

(A) 運ぶ
(B) さわる
(C) 与える

5. それはざらざらしているのでも，固いのでもありません。ある物がこのようである場合，それを押すと簡単に形が変わります。赤ちゃんの肌はこのようです。それは何ですか？

(A) やわらかい
(B) さまざまな色の
(C) 軽い

6. あなたは誕生日に，ケーキのろうそくにこのことをします。口を使ってすることです。そのためには深く息を吸い込まなければなりません。あなたは何をしますか？

(A) 叫ぶ
(B) 歌う
(C) 息を吹きかける

7. これはとても楽しいことです。飛行機に乗ることもありますが，必ずそうするわけではありません。あなたはこれをするために他のある場所に行きます。それは何ですか？

(A) 飛ぶこと
(B) 揺れること
(C) 旅行すること

8. このような人はよい人です。このような人は他の人を幸せにします。このような人はあなたを助けてくれます。この人は＿＿＿人です。

(A) みにくい
(B) 怖い
(C) 親切な

Lesson 7

■ 重要ポイント

確認問題

1. Tuesday, March 19th, 1998
   (Tuesday, March Nineteenth, Nineteen Ninety-eight)
2. Saturday, November 25th, 2008
   Saturday, November Twenty-fifth, Two Thousand Eight / Twenty O Eight)

■ 練習問題

| 1. (A) | 2. (B) | 3. (C) |
| 4. (A) | 5. (B) | 6. (C) |

[1-3]

```
         トニーの卒業アルバム
      トニーについて読んでください！

   好きな映画              趣味
   ―宇宙                   ―野球
   ―冒険                   ―読書
   ―動物                   ―友達と遊ぶこと

   好きな科目              好きな本
   ―数学                   ―ハリー・ポッター
   ―理科                   ―おおきな木
   ―体育                   ―星の王子さま
```

1. トニーはどんな映画が好きですか？

   (A) 野生動物の話
   (B) 王子さまとお姫さまの話
   (C) お笑いの話

2. トニーはどんな科目が好きですか？

   (A) 英語
   (B) 数学
   (C) 美術

3. トニーが自由時間に楽しんでいることは何ですか？

   (A) お兄さんといっしょに遊ぶこと
   (B) サッカーをすること
   (C) 本を読むこと

[4-6]

ジェファーソン小学校 昼食メニュー メニューの中から選んでください！			
メイン	野菜	果物	飲み物
スパゲッティ	ニンジン	リンゴ	リンゴジュース
ご飯と豆	サラダ	オレンジ	オレンジジュース
チャーハン	セロリ	バナナ	冷水
牛肉スープ	ミニトマト	キウイフルーツ	牛乳

4. このメニューは何のためのものですか？
   (A) 昼食の時間のため
   (B) おやつの時間のため
   (C) 夕食の時間のため

5. 生徒たちはどんな野菜を食べることができますか？
   (A) タマネギ
   (B) ニンジン
   (C) ブロッコリー

6. メニューにない飲み物は何ですか？
   (A) オレンジジュース
   (B) 牛乳
   (C) アイスティー

■ ミニテスト

1. (B)	2. (A)	3. (C)	4. (B)
5. (A)	6. (C)	7. (B)	8. (B)

[1-4]

私の日課 エリザベス・ターナー	
8:30 - 8:45	登校
9:00 - 10:00	数学—宿題
10:00 - 11:00	体育
11:00 - 12:00	理科
12:00 - 12:30	昼食
12:45 - 1:00	休み時間
1:00 - 1:30	音楽
1:45 - 2:45	英語
2:45 - 3:00	バスに乗って家に帰る

1. この日課表を作成した人はだれですか？
   (A) 親
   (B) 生徒
   (C) 先生

2. 宿題があるのはどの授業ですか？
   (A) 数学
   (B) 理科
   (C) 英語

3. どの時間が一番短い時間ですか？
   (A) 昼食
   (B) 理科
   (C) 休み時間

4. この生徒はどうやって学校から家に帰りますか？
   (A) 歩いて
   (B) バスに乗って
   (C) 車に乗って

[5-8]

運動会！ ロングフェロー小学校 私たちの学校の年に一度の行事におこしください。 行われる競技 リレー競走／なわとび大会 2つのチームに分かれて行います。 全生徒が参加します。 あなたのお子さまの走る姿を見に来てください。 4月17日金曜日 午後1時〜4時 ロングフェロー小学校運動場

5. チームの数はいくつを予定していますか？
   (A) 2チーム
   (B) 3チーム
   (C) 4チーム

6. 行事にはだれが参加する予定ですか？
   (A) スポーツチームに所属する生徒
   (B) 生徒と親
   (C) 全生徒

7. 行事はどこで行われる予定ですか？
   (A) 学校の食堂
   (B) 学校の運動場
   (C) 学校の教室

8. 生徒がしない競技は何ですか？
   (A) リレー競走
   (B) サッカー
   (C) なわとび

Lesson 8

■ 重要ポイント

確認問題
1. Where　　2. Who　　3. What
4. Why　　　5. How　　6. When

■ 練習問題

1. (C)　　2. (C)　　3. (A)　　4. (B)

[1-2]

おばあちゃんへ

パパが，おばあちゃんが重い病気だと言っています。早く元気になってください。おばあちゃんの家に早くまた行って，この前したカードゲームをしたいです。おばあちゃんが病気だと遊べません。ぼくが病気のときはたくさんお水を飲みます。そのおかげでぼくは元気になるのだと思います。おばあちゃんもたくさんお水を飲んで休んでください。すぐに会いに行きます。

あなたの孫，トムより

1. トムは病気の時に何をしますか？
   (A) 手紙を書く
   (B) ゲームをする
   (C) 水をたくさん飲む

2. トムはだれにこの手紙を書いていますか？
   (A) 彼のお父さん
   (B) 彼の孫
   (C) 彼のおばあちゃん

[3-4]

世界にはたくさんの便利な道具があります。その1つがブーメランです。ブーメランは空中に投げる物で，投げた後に手にまた戻ってきます。大昔には人々はブーメランを狩りや，火をおこすときにも使いました。ブーメランはとても強力です。最近では，ブーメランは面白い遊び道具として使われています。お店でブーメランを買うことができます。

3. 以前は，人々はブーメランをどのようなときに使いましたか？
   (A) 狩りをするとき
   (B) 遊ぶとき
   (C) お店に行くとき

4. ブーメランは何をしますか？
   (A) とても遠くに飛んで行って，地面に落ちる。
   (B) 空中を飛んで戻ってくる。
   (C) 鳥の目印になる。

■ ミニテスト

1. (A)　　2. (C)　　3. (C)　　4. (B)

[1-2]

ジョンおじさんへ

（おじさんと行った）動物園がどれほど楽しかったかを伝えたいと思います。今回の休暇は本当に楽しみました。ライオンとトラを見たことは本当に楽しかったです。ああ，それからペンギンも忘れられません。ぼくはペンギンが泳ぐ姿を見たのがとりわけ気に入りました。ぼくは，すべてのぼくの旅行がみんな今回みたいに楽しければいいなと思います。そして，おじさんにまた早く会いたいです。ぼくを動物園に連れていってくださって，本当にありがとうございました。

心をこめて　アンドリューより

1. アンドリューはなぜジョンおじさんに手紙を書いているのですか？
   (A) 動物園に連れていってくれたお礼を言うため
   (B) おじさんが動物園に行きたいかどうか確かめるため
   (C) おじさんへの誕生日祝いのメッセージを伝えるため

2. アンドリューは何がとりわけ気に入りましたか？
   (A) ライオン
   (B) トラ
   (C) ペンギン

[3-4]

ぼくが一番好きなおもちゃはスケートボードだ。スケートボードはぼくの11歳の誕生日にプレゼントでもらったものだ。夏の間スケートボードに乗る。ぼくは公園でそれに乗るのが大好きで，スケートボードでいくつかのすてきな技をすることができる。ボードからとんだり，円を描いて回ることもできる。ぼくのスケートボードは赤いしま模様が入った青いボードだ。どちらも大好きな色だ。ぼくは友達ともスケートボードに乗れる。本当に楽しいよ。

3. この子どもができない技は何ですか？
   (A) ボードからとぶこと
   (B) 円を描いて回ること
   (C) 車をとびこえること

4. この子どもがスケートボードを乗るのに好きな場所はどこですか？
   (A) 友達の家
   (B) 公園
   (C) 歩道

Lesson 9

■ 重要ポイント

やってみよう！
an apple, a banana / difficult, study

■ 練習問題

| 1. (C) | 2. (B) | 3. (B) | 4. (A) |
| 5. (C) | 6. (C) | 7. (B) | 8. (A) |

1. The pig has a ribbon around its neck.
   そのブタは首のまわりにリボンをつけています。

2. The man is holding some presents.
   その男の人はプレゼントをいくつか抱えています。

3. A couple walks their dogs.
   カップルが犬に散歩をさせます。

4. In the middle of the pond, there is an alligator.
   池の中央にワニがいます。

5. The road is empty.
   道路がすいています。

6. The lady is wearing a pair of glasses.
   その女性はメガネをかけています。

7. They are both looking at the same skirt.
   彼女たちは2人とも同じスカートを見ています。

8. He sat next to his sister instead of his grandmother.
   彼はおばあさんのとなりではなく、妹の横に座りました。

■ ミニテスト

| 1. (C) | 2. (C) | 3. (B) | 4. (A) |
| 5. (B) | 6. (A) | 7. (C) | 8. (B) |

1. There ¹are three ²candles on a cake.
   ケーキの上に3本のろうそくがある。

2. The man is ³petting his cat.
   男の人がネコをなでている。

3. She is too ⁴small for the sweater.
   彼女はそのセーターを着るには小さすぎる。

4. She ⁵turned off the television.
   彼女はテレビを消した。

5. The boy ⁶hurt his knee.
   男の子はひざをけがした。

6. He ⁷won first ⁸place in the singing contest.
   彼はのど自慢大会で優勝した。

7. The little girl is too ⁹scared to ¹⁰see the snake.
   小さな女の子は怖くてヘビを見ることができない。

8. The blue cup is ¹¹smaller than the yellow cup, but it is ¹²bigger than the red cup.
   青いコップは黄色いカップより小さいが、赤いカップより大きい。

Lesson 10

■ 重要ポイント

やってみよう！
ride a bicycle (bike) / say goodbye

■ 練習問題

| 1. (B) | 2. (A) | 3. (C) | 4. (B) |
| 5. (A) | 6. (A) | 7. (C) | 8. (B) |

1. W: Choose a partner. Play and listen to the CD together. The song will play two times.
   相手を選んで、CDをかけていっしょに聞いてください。歌は2度流れます。

2. W: Please do not yell so loudly in class. It hurts the other students' ears.
   授業中にそんなに大声で叫ばないでください。それは他の生徒の耳を傷めます。

3. M: It is a very sunny day outside. Remember to turn off the lights in your bedroom when you are not in the room. Doing this will save energy.
   外はとてもいい天気です。部屋にいないときは忘れずに寝室の電気を消しましょう。そうすればエネルギーが節約できます。

4. M: Our science lesson for today is about frogs. I would like you to choose a partner and share a notebook. Each one of you will get a book about frogs.
今日，私たちの理科の授業ではカエルについて学びます。それでは，パートナーを選んでいっしょにノートを取ってください。みなさんには各自カエルに関する本を配布します。

5. W: Painting can sometimes be very messy. Please be careful and only paint on your paper. Do not get any paint on your desk.
絵の具で絵を描くと，まわりをひどくよごしてしまうことがあります。みなさんは注意して紙の上にだけ描くようにしてください。机に絵の具をこぼさないようにしてください。

6. B: Sally, give me back my green toy cars! You took them from the big toy box without asking. I want to play with them now.
サリー，ぼくの緑色のおもちゃの車を返してよ。君はぼくに聞きもしないで大きなおもちゃ箱から持って行っただろう。ぼくは今それで遊びたいんだ。

7. W: Today I would like to introduce a new student. He just moved to town and doesn't know anyone. I want each of you to come to the front of the classroom. And write your name on the board, so he knows who you are.
今日は新しい生徒を紹介したいと思います。彼は引っ越してきたばかりで知り合いがいません。では，みなさんは1人ずつ前に出てください。黒板にみなさんの名前を書いてみなさんがだれなのか彼に知らせてください。

8. M: Ben, you need to start eating healthy foods like fruits and vegetables. Your test results show that you have too much sugar in your body. I will help you plan a healthier diet.
ベン，これからは果物や野菜のような健康によい食べ物を食べ始めなければならないよ。君の検査結果を見ると君の体には，糖分がとても多い。君がもっと健康な食事計画を立てられるようぼくが手伝ってあげるよ。

■ ミニテスト

| 1. (A) | 2. (B) | 3. (C) | 4. (A) |
| 5. (C) | 6. (C) | 7. (B) | 8. (C) |

1. W: Now it's time to ¹finish the test. Raise your hand if you're finished writing all your answers.
さあ，試験の終わる時間ですよ。答えをすべて書き終えたら手をあげてください。

2. W: We are going to go for a long walk. Please ²put on your running shoes that are sitting by the door.
私たちはこれから遠くまで散歩に出かけます。ドアのそばに置いておいた運動靴をはきましょう。

3. M: I am getting very old. Sometimes I need help. Can you please ³come over here and help me out of my chair? Just ⁴take my hand while I try to stand up.
私はもうずいぶん年をとった。時には助けが必要だ。こちらに来て私がいすから立つのを手伝っておくれ。私が立ち上がる間私の手をつかんでおいてくれればいい。

4. M: Today, we will ⁵learn about wild animals. Please sit with your hands in your lap and watch this video. It will not ⁶take a very long time.
今日は野生動物について学びます。ひざの上に両手を置いて座ってこのビデオを見てください。あまり長くはかかりません。

5. W: Sam, your teeth look very yellow. You should try ⁷brushing your teeth with this toothpaste. Here is a new toothbrush too.
サム，歯がとても黄色く見えるわよ。この歯磨きを使ってみて。新しい歯ブラシもここにあるわ。

6. W: Stop running in the hallway! You need to calm down and walk slowly. If you are running too fast, you might accidentally ⁸bump into another student or teacher.
廊下で走るのをやめなさい！静かにしてゆっくり歩かなければなりません。あまりにも速く走れば，偶然他の生徒や先生とぶつかってしまうかもしれません。

7. M: To help you memorize your vocabulary words, we're going to make flashcards. Please write the ⁹word on the front of the card and write the ¹⁰meaning of the word on the back of the card. These flashcards will help you during your quiz.
単語の暗記をするために，私たちはフラッシュカードを作ります。カードの表には単語を書いて，カードの裏側にはその意味を書くようにしてください。このフラッシュカードが小テストのときに役に立ちます。

8. M: Hey, I can see the spaghetti noodles in your mouth. Please ¹¹chew your food with your mouth closed. If your mouth ¹²is open while you eat, everyone can see the chewed food, and it is very noisy.
おや，君の口の中にあるスパゲッティが丸見えだ。食べ物をかむときは口を閉じてくれ。食べている途中に口を開けたら，だれにも君がかんでいる食べ物が見えてしまって，とても見苦しいよ。

Lesson 11

■ 重要ポイント

やってみよう！
driving / he is a teacher

■ 練習問題

| 1. (A) | 2. (C) | 3. (B) | 4. (A) |
| 5. (C) | 6. (B) | 7. (B) | 8. (C) |

1. M: Did you bring your backpack today?
   今日はランドセルを持ってきたかい？

   (A) Yes, it is by the door.
   　　はい，ドアの横にあります。
   (B) No, I can't go today.　いいえ，今日は行けません。
   (C) Yes, it looks good.　はい，それは格好いいです。

2. M: Have you finished your homework?
   君は宿題を終わらせたのかい？

   (A) Yes, I will go soon.　はい，すぐ行きます。
   (B) I am good at doing homework.　私は宿題をするのが得意です。
   (C) No, I didn't know two answers.
   　　いいえ，問題のうち2つがわかりませんでした。

3. M: How was swim practice today?
   今日の水泳の練習はどうだった？

   (A) No, thank you.　いいえ，結構です。
   (B) Good, I swam fast.
   　　よかったです。私は速く泳げました。
   (C) I like our swimming pool.
   　　私は私たちのプールが好きです。

4. M: Do you think you can win the race?
   君はその競技で勝てると思うかい？

   (A) I will try my best.　最善を尽くします。
   (B) It's not too bad.　そんなに悪くはないです。
   (C) OK, I won't.　わかりました，もうしません。

5. W: How did you fall down and scratch your knee?
   どうして転んでひざをすりむいたりしたの？

   (A) No, I don't need a bandage.
   　　いいえ，包帯はいりません。
   (B) Please, it hurts a lot.
   　　お願いします。すごく痛いんです。
   (C) I tripped on the stairs.　階段でつまずいたのです。

6. W: Let's wrap up your knee, so you can go back to class.
   授業に戻れるように，ひざに包帯を巻きましょう。

   (A) It looks interesting.　面白そうですね。
   (B) OK, that sounds good.
   　　はい，それがよさそうですね。
   (C) Thank you, I did my best.
   　　ありがとう，私は最善を尽くしましたよ。

7. W: What kind of books do you like to read?
   どんな種類の本を読みたいですか？

   (A) I like to ride my bicycle.
   　　私は自転車に乗るのが好きです。
   (B) I like books that are funny.
   　　私は楽しい本が好きです。
   (C) Adventure books scare me.
   　　冒険に関する本は怖いです。

8. W: Can I please see your library card?
   あなたの図書貸し出しカードを見せていただけますか？

   (A) The desk is over there.　机はそちらにあります。
   (B) Yes, I can see that.
   　　はい，私はそれを見ることができます。
   (C) Oh, I left it at home.
   　　おや，私はそれを家に忘れてしまいました。

■ ミニテスト

| 1. (B) | 2. (A) | 3. (B) | 4. (C) |
| 5. (B) | 6. (C) | 7. (B) | 8. (A) |

1. G: Which one is your locker?
   どれがあなたのロッカーなの？

   (A) I am right-handed.　私は右ききです。
   (B) The one ¹on the left.　左側にあるほうです。
   (C) Please walk forward.　前に向かって歩いてください。

2. G: Can you ²help me carry my books to class?
   私の本を教室に運ぶのを手伝ってくれる？

   (A) Sure, I can help you.　もちろん手伝うよ。
   (B) Yes, I have many books.
   　　はい，私は本をたくさん持っています。
   (C) The history book ³is heavy.　歴史の本は重いです。

3. M: Where do you live?
   あなたはどこに住んでいますか？

   (A) Please stop the bus.　バスを止めてください。
   (B) Just ⁴down the street.
   　　その道を真っすぐ行ったところです。
   (C) You are a good driver.　あなたはよい運転手ですね。

4. M: Please find a seat and sit down.
   席を見つけて座ってください。

(A) I can't see anything. 私には何も見えません。
(B) It's very cold ⁵in here. ここはとても寒いです。
(C) But all the seats ⁶are full.
でも席はすべてうまっています。

5. W: Please ⁷sit down at this table to read.
このテーブルの席に座って読んでください。

(A) I like my reading teacher.
私はリーディングの先生が好きです。
(B) Thank you, I will. ありがとう，そうします。
(C) I can't decide. 私は決められません。

6. W: Is this book ⁸hard to read?
この本は読むのが難しいですか？

(A) No, I can't look right now.
いいえ，今は見ることができません。
(B) Maybe, it's hard to ⁹choose just one.
たぶん，1つだけ選ぶことは難しいです。
(C) Yes, the book is very hard to understand.
はい，その本を理解するのはとても難しいです。

7. M: ¹⁰How much do you know about math?
数学についてどれくらい知っていますか？

(A) I think there are too many.
とてもたくさんあるようです。
(B) I don't really ¹¹know a lot.
それほどよく知っているわけではありません。
(C) That sounds fun. 面白そうですね。

8. M: Can you answer this math problem?
あなたはこの数学の問題に答えられますか？

(A) Sure, ¹²I can try. はい，やってみます。
(B) I read it last week. 私はそれを先週読みました。
(C) I said many things.
私はたくさんのことを言いました。

Lesson 12

■ 重要ポイント

やってみよう！
go camping with us / his father

■ 練習問題

| 1. (B) | 2. (A) | 3. (A) | 4. (C) |
| 5. (C) | 6. (B) | 7. (C) | 8. (A) |

1. W: How are you feeling today?
今日の体の具合はどうですか？

(A) Just a little. 少しだけ。
(B) I have a headache. 頭痛がします。
(C) Yes, it's a sunny day. はい，いい天気ですね。

2. W: Why does your head hurt?
あなたはなぜ頭が痛いのですか？

(A) I bumped it on a corner. 角に頭をぶつけたんです。
(B) I need to lie down. 私は寝なければなりません。
(C) Yes, I feel dizzy. はい，めまいがします。

3. M: Don't trip and fall. Please watch your step.
踏み外して転ばないように，足元に気をつけてください。

(A) OK, thank you for telling me.
はい，教えてくれてありがとう。
(B) I think I can jump down.
私は飛び降りることができると思います。
(C) Please come over here. こっちに来てください。

4. M: Will you please scan your bus card?
バスカードをスキャンしていただけますか？

(A) Thank you for your time.
時間を取ってくれてありがとう。
(B) It is good to see you. あなたに会えてよかった。
(C) I am going to. そうします。

5. W: Which puppy do you like?
あなたはどちらの子犬が好きですか？

(A) His fur is very fluffy.
その毛はとてもふわふわしています。
(B) She looks so cute sleeping.
彼女の寝ている姿はとてもかわいいです。
(C) I like the small, brown one.
小さくて茶色いのが好きです。

6. W: Would you like to hold the puppy?
子犬をだいてみたいですか？

(A) Yes, I heard them talking.

14

はい，彼らが話しているのを聞きました。

(B) Yes, please give it to me.
　　はい，私に渡してください。

(C) Yes, I will ask right now.
　　はい，今すぐ聞いてみます。

7. M: I like that sweater you are wearing.
　　あなたが着ているセーター，いいわね。

(A) No, thank you. I can do it.
　　いいえ，大丈夫です。私でもできます。

(B) My mom can help me.
　　私のお母さんが手伝ってくれます。

(C) Thank you, it's my favorite.
　　ありがとう，私のお気に入りなんです。

8. M: Would you like to try the coat on?
　　このコートを着てみますか？

(A) Yes, but show me another color.
　　はい，しかし他の色を見せてください。

(B) It is very cold outside today.
　　今日は外がとても寒いです。

(C) It is a little expensive for me.　私には少し高いです。

■ ミニテスト

| 1. (B) | 2. (C) | 3. (B) | 4. (B) |
| 5. (A) | 6. (C) | 7. (A) | 8. (C) |

1. M: Hello there, ¹how can I help you?
　　こんにちは，今日はどうしましたか？

(A) Yes, it's on the table.
　　はい，それはテーブルの上にあります。

(B) Hi, my cat is very sick.
　　こんにちは，私のネコがひどく具合が悪いんです。

(C) Now I feel happy.　今私は幸福です。

2. M: I think your cat will ²feel fine in a few days.
　　あなたのネコは数日でよくなると思います。

(A) I feel very sad today.　私は今日，とても悲しいです。

(B) You are ³very kind to me.
　　あなたはとても私に優しいですね。

(C) Thank you, I was worried.
　　ありがとうございます，心配していました。

3. W: Hey, I ⁴have a job for you.
　　ねえ，あなたにしてもらいたい仕事があるの。

(A) I can't remember.　思い出せない。

(B) Oh really? What is it?　本当？それは何？

(C) Do you like your job?
　　あなたは自分の仕事が好きですか？

4. W: Can you please ⁵water the flowers for me?
　　私の代わりに花に水をやってくれる？

(A) OK, I won't.　いいよ，しません。

(B) Yes, I certainly will.　わかった，必ずやりますよ。

(C) You can ⁶come to see me.　会いに来ていいよ。

5. W: Would you like ⁷some ice cream for dessert?
　　デザートにアイスクリームを少しいかがですか？

(A) Sure, that sounds good.　もちろん，お願いします。

(B) I cannot go there.　私はそこに行けません。

(C) No, I don't like you.
　　いいえ，私はあなたが嫌いです。

6. W: What flavor of ice cream do you want?
　　どんな味のアイスクリームになさいますか？

(A) ⁸Just two please.　2つだけください。

(B) ⁹Pass me the sugar.　砂糖をちょっと取ってください。

(C) I will have chocolate.　チョコレート味にします。

7. W: Welcome to Dazzling Dresses. There is a ¹⁰big sale on dresses today.
　　Dazzling Dressesへようこそ。今日はドレスの大セールがあります。

(A) Great, I love sales.
　　いいですね，私はセールが大好きなんです。

(B) There is a 50% discount.　50%引です。

(C) I heard him ¹¹on the radio.
　　ラジオで彼の声を聞きました。

8. W: It ¹²looks like you found the perfect dress.
　　あなたは完ぺきなドレスを見つけたようですね。

(A) I can't find the zipper.　ジッパーが見つかりません。

(B) No, his pants are too big.
　　いいえ，彼のズボンは大きすぎます。

(C) I agree. This dress is very lovely.
　　同感です。このドレスはとてもかわいいです。

Lesson 13

■ 重要ポイント

やってみよう！
call your friend / didn't do my homework

■ 練習問題

| 1. (B) | 2. (B) | 3. (C) | 4. (C) |
| 5. (B) | 6. (A) | 7. (C) | 8. (A) |

1. M: Will you please hang up your jacket?
   G: Where should I hang it up?
   M: On a hook over there in the closet.
   G: OK, sounds good.

   M: 君の上着は掛けておいてくれますか？
   G: どこに掛ければいいでしょうか？
   M: あそこのクローゼットの中のフックに。
   G: はい，わかりました。

   女の子は次に何をしますか？
   (A) フックをクローゼットに取りつける
   (B) 上着をクローゼットにしまう
   (C) ランドセルをドアのそばに掛ける

2. W: Can I help you find a book?
   B: Yes, I have to do a research project on bears.
   W: Oh fun, we have a bunch of bear books over there.
   B: Thanks, I will go and look at them.

   W: 本を探すのを手伝いましょうか？
   B: はい，クマに関する研究課題をしなければならないんです。
   W: あら，楽しそうですね。そちらにクマに関する本がたくさんありますよ。
   B: ありがとう，行って見てみます。

   男の子は次に何をしますか？
   (A) テーブルのいすに座る
   (B) クマについての本を見つける
   (C) 彼の研究課題を終わらせる

3. M: Welcome to the first day of school. Please make a name tag right away.
   G: Why do we need to make a name tag?
   M: Because then every student can know your name. It is very helpful.
   G: Oh I see. It is good to know everyone's name.
   M: Of course, that's why I want you to make a name tag.

   M: ようこそ，今日が最初の登校日です。すぐに名札を作ってください。
   G: なぜ名札を作らないといけないのですか？
   M: そうすればクラスのみんながあなたの名前を知ることができます。それはとても役に立ちますよ。
   G: はい，わかりました。みんなの名前がわかるといいですね。
   M: そのとおり，だからあなたに名札を作ってもらいたいのです。

   女の子はなぜ名札が必要なのですか？
   (A) 彼女の宿題のためです。
   (B) 学校の最後の日だからです。
   (C) そうすればクラスの友達が彼女の名前を知ることができるからです。

4. G1: Is the book you're reading interesting?
   G2: It sure is. It's an action book full of adventure.
   G1: Cool. I'm kind of hungry. Do you know when lunch time is?
   G2: I think we will have lunch in the cafeteria really soon, when the next bell rings.
   G1: Good, I hope they serve us pizza today.

   G1: あなたが読んでいる本は面白いのですか？
   G2: すごく面白いわ。冒険いっぱいのアクション小説よ。
   G1: かっこいい。私は少しおなかが空いちゃった。昼食の時間はいつだか知ってる？
   G2: もうすぐよ，次のチャイムが鳴ったら食堂で昼食よ。
   G1: よかった，今日はピザが出るといいな。

   女の子たちは次に何をしますか？
   (A) もっとたくさんのアクション小説を読む
   (B) ピザを食べに家に行く
   (C) 食堂に行く

5. W: I am glad you got to practice painting your partner's face.
   B: It was very hard to do. I don't think my painting looks like my partner.
   W: What are you talking about? It looks exactly like him. Good job!
   B: Thanks, but now my brushes are covered in paint.
   W: Well I suggest you wash them out in the sink.

   W: あなたがペアになった相手の顔を描く練習をするようになってうれしいわ。
   B: 大変でした。ぼくの絵は，ぼくの相手のようにはとても見えないでしょう。
   W: そんなことないわ。彼とそっくり同じに見えるわよ。よくできたと思うわ。
   B: ありがとうございます。でももう筆が絵の具でよごれてしまいました。

W: それなら，流しで洗うといいわよ。

男の子は次に何をしますか？
(A) 新しい絵筆を持ってくる
(B) 絵筆を洗う
(C) ペアになった相手の顔を絵の具で描く

6. G: I'm nervous for music class. I'm not a very good singer.
   B: Oh, don't worry. I think you'll do just fine.
   G: But one time, I tried singing in class, and everyone laughed at me.
   B: Oh, forget it. They are just being mean.
   G: I don't know. I am just scared that I will make mistakes again.

G: 音楽の授業は気が重いわ。私は歌があまりうまくないから。
B: まあ，心配するなよ。ぼくは君がうまくこなせると思うよ。
G: でも一度，授業で歌ってみたんだけど，みんなが私を笑ったの。
B: そんなの忘れろよ。彼らはちょっと意地悪してるだけさ。
G: そうかな。でも，また間違えちゃうんじゃないかと思うと怖くて。

女の子はなぜ歌を歌いたくないのですか？
(A) 歌うのに緊張するから。
(B) 先生が彼女を嫌っているから。
(C) 絵を描くほうが上手だから。

7. G: Hey, do you know when our next school field trip is? I forgot.
   B: I'm not sure. Maybe you should look at the school calendar.
   G: Good idea. Oh wait, it says the field trip is in October, but it doesn't say where.
   B: Then why don't you ask the teacher where our next field trip will be?
   G: OK, I will ask the teacher.

G: ねえ，次の遠足がいつあるのか知ってる？　私忘れちゃった。
B: どうだったかな。学校のカレンダーを見てみたらどう？
G: いい考えね。あ，ちょっと待って，遠足は10月だと書いてあるけど，どこに行くかは書いてないわ。
B: じゃあ次の遠足でどこに行くか先生に聞いてみたら？
G: うん，先生に聞いてみる。

女の子は次に何をしますか？
(A) カレンダーを見る
(B) 次の遠足を計画する
(C) 先生に質問する

8. M: In your journal, please write about your favorite teacher.
   B: Can I write about any teacher in the school? Like the math teacher, Mr. Todd?
   M: Yes, you can choose any teacher you like.
   B: I don't really like math. I like doing science experiments. But what I enjoy the most is painting and drawing.
   M: Great. Mrs. Honey is a really good teacher.
   B: I think so too. I'll write about her.

M: あなたが一番好きな先生について，日記に書いてください。
B: 学校にいらっしゃる先生であればだれについて書いてもいいのですか？　たとえば数学のトッド先生でも？
M: そうです。だれでもあなたが好きな先生を選んでください。
B: ぼくは数学があまり好きではありません。ぼくは理科の実験が好きです。でも一番楽しいのは絵の具をぬったり絵を描いたりすることです。
M: いいですね。ハニー先生は本当にすばらしい先生です。
B: ぼくもそう思います。その先生について書こうと思います。

男の子は何をしたいと思っていますか？
(A) 美術の先生について書く
(B) 数学の先生について書く
(C) 理科の実験について書く

■ ミニテスト

| 1. (C) | 2. (B) | 3. (B) | 4. (C) |
| 5. (B) | 6. (A) | 7. (C) | 8. (B) |

1. W: Our art project today is to make a clay cup.
   G: Can I make a bowl ¹instead of a cup, please?
   W: ²I don't think that is a good idea.
   G: Please, I think it would turn out really well.

W: 今日の私たちの美術の課題は，粘土でカップを作ることです。
G: 私はカップの代わりにおわんを作ってもいいですか？
W: いい考えではないと思います。
G: お願いします，そうすれば本当にいいものが作れる気がするんです。

女の子は何をしたがっていますか？
(A) 美術の時間に絵を描く
(B) きれいなカップを描く
(C) 粘土のおわんを作る

解答・解説 Step 1　17

2. M: Today we are going to run around the track four times.
   B: Oh, I didn't know we were doing that today. I'll switch my shoes.
   M: Why do you need to do that?
   B: Because the shoes I'm wearing are ³not for running.

   M: 今日はみんなでトラックを4周するぞ。
   B: ええっ，今日そんなことをするなんて知らなかった。靴をかえます。
   M: なぜだい？
   B: 今はいている靴は走るのには向いていないからです。

   男の子は次に何をしますか？
   (A) 靴ひもを結ぶ
   (B) 靴をはきかえる
   (C) トラックを走ってまわる

3. W: Are you ⁴looking for something? Do you need my help?
   G: I need to find a video and a book on farm animals.
   W: Oh, well I see you found a book about farm animals.
   G: Yes, I did. Now I just need to find a video ⁵on the same topic.
   W: We keep all videos in the video room. If you can't find it, just come to me again.

   W: 何かを探しているの？　手伝いましょうか？
   G: 家畜についてのビデオと本を見つけないといけないんです。
   W: あら，家畜についての本は見つけたみたいですね。
   G: はい，見つけました。あとは同じ主題についてのビデオを見つければいいだけです。
   W: ビデオはみんなビデオ室に保管されています。見つからなければまた私のところに来てください。

   女の子は次にどこに行きますか？
   (A) トイレに
   (B) ビデオ室に
   (C) 映画館に

4. G1: Are you ready for our English test tomorrow?
   G2: No, are you?
   G1: Yeah, but I can't understand the review handout. Do you get it?
   G2: Not really, I think it's really hard. Do you want to ⁶study together tonight?
   G1: Yes, that would be great.

   G1: 明日の英語の試験，準備はできてる？
   G2: いいえ，あなたは？
   G1: できたわ。でも復習プリントがわからないの。あなたはわかる？
   G2: あんまり。あれはかなり難しいと思うわ。今夜いっしょに勉強する？
   G1: ええ，それがよさそうね。

   女の子たちは何をしようとしていますか？
   (A) 復習ゲームをする
   (B) 教室でとなり同士に座る
   (C) いっしょに試験勉強をする

5. W: So tell me, why do you have such a bad headache?
   B: I was trying to reach up and get a book on the top shelf.
   W: Let me guess. You accidently knocked down several books.
   B: Yes, many books fell, and one really big book ⁷hit my head.
   W: I can see that from the bump on the back of your head. Let's ⁸put some ice on it.

   W: それで，教えてちょうだい。なぜそんなに頭が痛いの？
   B: 一番上の棚にある本を取ろうとして背伸びをしたんです。
   W: 当ててみましょう。間違って本を何冊か落としてしまったのですね。
   B: はい，たくさん本が落ちて，すごく大きな本がぼくの頭に当たったんです
   W: あなたの頭の後ろ側にこぶができているからそうとわかるわ。そこに氷を当てましょう。

   男の子はなぜ頭がひどく痛むのですか？
   (A) あまりに高くジャンプしたから。
   (B) 本が彼の頭に落ちてきたから。
   (C) はしごから落ちたから。

6. M: Thank you for bringing me these paper towels.
   G: You're welcome. My teacher reminded me to after class. She said you needed them as soon as possible.
   M: Good, I'm glad you did that. It's always nice to talk to students.
   G: I'd like to say thank you for all you do for our school. You ⁹keep everything so clean!
   M: Of course, that's my job. And I really like that you care.

   M: ペーパータオルを持ってきてくれてありがとう。
   G: どういたしまして。授業の後に先生から言いつけられたんです。今すぐにでも必要だからって。
   M: すばらしい。持ってきてくれてうれしいよ。生徒と話

G: こちらこそ私たちの学校のためにいろいろしてくれてお礼を言いたいです。すべてをこんなにきれいにしてくれてるんだもの。
M: もちろん，それがぼくの仕事だからね。でもそんなふうに気づかってくれるのは本当にうれしいよ。

女の子は何をすることを覚えていたのですか？

(A) 用務員にタオルを持っていくこと
(B) 机を掃除すること
(C) 職員室に行くこと

7. W: Now, let's open our books to page seven and ¹⁰begin reading.
B: Before we start reading, may I please get a drink of water out in the hallway? I am very thirsty.
W: Oh, you can use the sink in the classroom to get water. But please be quick.
B: OK, thank you.
W: Be sure to use a paper cup to drink the water.

W: では，本の7ページを開いて，朗読を始めてください。
B: 読み始める前に，廊下に出て水を飲みに行ってもいいですか？ とてものどがかわいているんです。
W: そうですか，教室の流し台で水を飲んでもかまいませんよ。でも早くしてくださいね。
B: はい，ありがとうございます。
W: 必ず紙コップを使って飲むんですよ。

男の子はどのように水を飲みますか？

(A) ボトルの水を買って
(B) 廊下にある水飲み器から
(C) 流し台の水を使って

8. M: I like how neatly you can stack all of the building blocks together.
G: Thank you. I really like playing with the building blocks. They are ¹¹fun to play with.
M: You should ¹²try making a tall building with them. Like the buildings outside of the school.
G: Hmm, I think I would rather build a house that looks exactly like mine.
M: Oh that's a brilliant idea. I'm sure it will be really fun to build.

M: ブロックを積んで建物を作るのが本当に上手だね。
G: ありがとう。ブロックで遊ぶのは大好き。使って遊ぶと面白いの。
M: それを使って高いビルを作ってみたらどうかな。たとえば，学校の外にあるようなビルなんかを。
G: ううん，それよりも私の家とそっくり同じ形の家を作ってみたいわ。
M: なるほど，それはすばらしい考えだ。きっと面白いと思うよ。

女の子は何をしたいと言っていますか？

(A) 高いビルを作る
(B) 自分の家のような家を作る
(C) ブロックを片づける

Lesson 14

■ 重要ポイント

やってみよう！
a good idea / play with

■ 練習問題

1. (A)	2. (C)	3. (B)	4. (B)
5. (C)	6. (A)	7. (B)	8. (B)

1. W: Do you want to see a scary movie?
   B: No, I would be too frightened. I would rather see a funny one.
   W: OK, that works too. Do you want anything to eat?
   B: Sure, I'm hungry for some popcorn.

   W: 怖い映画を見たい？
   B: 嫌だよ，とても怖くなりそうだから。それより楽しい映画がいい。
   W: そう，それでもいいわ。何か食べたい？
   B: うん，ポップコーンを食べたいよ。

   息子は何をしたいと言っていますか？
   (A) 面白い映画を見る
   (B) 映画を見るためにキャンディーを買う
   (C) お母さんといっしょに怖い映画を見る

2. M: I have your results back, and your leg is broken.
   G: Oh no, that's why it hurt so much.
   M: How did you break your leg?
   G: I tried climbing a pretty big tree and fell.
   M: Next time, you should be more careful.

   M: 検査結果が出ました。足が折れていますね。
   G: ああ，だからこんなに痛かったのね。
   M: どうして折ってしまったのですか。
   G: かなり大きな木に登ろうとして落ちてしまったんです。
   M: 今度からはもっと気をつけなければいけませんね。

   女の子はどうして足を折ってしまったのですか？
   (A) 放課後になわとびをしていて。
   (B) 自転車に乗っているときに転んで。
   (C) 木登りをしているときに落ちて。

3. G: I really like these shoes. What do you think of them?
   B: Those are really cool colors, and they look very comfortable to wear.
   G: I agree. Blue and green are my favorite. Do you think I should try them on?
   B: Sure, why not? What is your shoe size?
   G: I am a size six. Please hand me that pair over there.

   G: この靴，すごく気に入ったわ。これどう思う？
   B: 色もすごくかっこいいし，はきやすそうだね。
   G: 私もそう思う。青と緑は好きな色なの。試しにはいてみたほうがいいと思う？
   B: もちろんそうするべきだよ。靴のサイズはいくつ？
   G: 私のサイズは6よ。そこにある靴を取ってくれる？

   女の子は次に何をするでしょうか？
   (A) 彼女のサイズの靴を頼む
   (B) 靴をはいてみる
   (C) 走りに行く

4. M: Hi, it looks like your neighbors are not home. Could you give them this package for me?
   B: OK, but I'm not sure what time they will be back home.
   M: Don't worry. I will write a note and put it on their door saying you have it.
   B: That sounds like a good plan. I will be sure to give them the package.
   M: Thank you for your help. Have a good day.

   M: こんにちは。おとなりの方が家にいらっしゃらないようなんです。この小包を私の代わりに渡していただけますか。
   B: かまいませんが，彼らがいつ帰ってくるのか，ぼくは知りませんよ。
   M: 大丈夫です。あなたが預かっていることをメモに書いて彼らのドアにはっておきますから。
   B: いい考えですね。必ず彼らに小包を渡しますよ。
   M: ご協力ありがとうございます。よい一日を。

   男の子は何をしようとしていますか？
   (A) 彼のおとなりさんに手紙を書く
   (B) 彼のおとなりさんに小包を渡す
   (C) 郵便配達員を手伝って彼のおとなりさんを探す

5. W: I think that hat looks good on you.
   B: Thanks, but I'm looking for a good birthday present for my friend.
   W: Oh, that's really nice of you. Well I still think that hat would be a great birthday present.
   B: Yeah, I'm sure my friend would like it. How much does it cost?
   W: It costs $20.00, but I will give you a discount because it's a present.
   B: OK, I'll buy it.

   W: その帽子はお客様によくお似合いですよ。

B: ありがとう，でも友達の誕生日プレゼントを探してるんです。
W: なるほど，優しいんですね。やはり私はその帽子がすばらしい誕生日プレゼントになると思いますよ。
B: ええ，ぼくの友達も気に入ると思います。いくらですか？
W: 20ドルです。でもプレゼントということだから，値引きしましょう。
B: よかった，それを買います。

男の子はなぜその帽子を買うのですか？
(A) それを使って遊ぶため
(B) 自分のために取っておくため
(C) 友達に贈るため

6. M: How was the movie with your friends?
G: It was really fun! I think next weekend we will go to another one.
M: Good, I am glad you're hanging out with your friends.
G: Yeah, but now I'm really tired. I think I'm going to get some sleep.
M: That sounds like a good idea.

M: 友達と見に行った映画はどうだった？
G: すごく面白かった！ 来週末また他の作品を見に行こうと思うわ。
M: よかったな。お前が友達と仲よくやってるみたいで，私もうれしいよ。
G: うん，でもすごく疲れちゃった。ちょっと休むわ。
M: いい考えだね。

娘はこれから何をするつもりですか？
(A) 休む
(B) 映画に行く
(C) 友達と遊ぶ

7. M: Time to wake up from your nap. I know my driving can be pretty smooth.
G: Oh sorry. School was very tiring today.
M: Not a problem. I just need to know where I can drop you off. I want it to be close to your house, so you don't have to walk far.
G: Thank you. But I don't mind walking. You can drop me off right here on the corner.
M: Sounds good. Be safe.

M: そろそろ起きてください。私の運転がスムーズすぎましたかね。
G: あ，ごめんなさい，今日は学校が本当に大変だったんです。
M: 大丈夫ですよ。どこで降ろせばいいのか，教えてください。おうちの近くに停めたいと思いまして。そうす

ればあなたも長く歩かなくてすむでしょう。
G: ありがとうございます。でも大丈夫ですよ。ちょうどその曲がり角のところで降ろしてくださってかまいません。
M: わかりました。お気をつけて。

女の子はどうやって家に帰りますか？
(A) 地下鉄に乗って家に帰ります。
(B) 残りの道を歩いて帰ります。
(C) バスの運転手が家まで送って行きます。

8. W: Welcome to Skates on Ice.
B: Hi. I'm here with my mom. We want to look at ice skates today.
W: Well that sounds wonderful. It's the perfect time of year to go ice skating.
B: That's exactly what I want to do. I want to bring my sister with me too.
W: Well that's very kind of you. I'm sure your sister will love spending time with you.

W: Skates on Iceにようこそ。
B: こんにちは，母といっしょに来ました。今日はスケート靴を見たいんです。
W: それはすばらしい。今はスケートをするのに絶好の時期ですよ。
B: ええ，それこそぼくがやりたいことなんです。妹も連れて行きたいと思っています。
W: 優しいお兄さんですね。妹さんもきっとあなたといっしょに時間を過ごすことを喜ばれるでしょう。

男の子はどうしてスケート靴がほしいのですか？
(A) 友達といっしょに遊ぶため
(B) 妹とスケートをしに行くため
(C) 妹の誕生日プレゼントに贈るため

■ **ミニテスト**

| 1. (C) | 2. (A) | 3. (A) | 4. (C) |
| 5. (A) | 6. (B) | 7. (B) | 8. (C) |

1. B: How come I have so much ice cream?
G: Because you asked for two big scoops instead of one.
B: Oh that's ¹too much for me. Now, I need a spoon to eat it.
G: I think you might need a couple of napkins too!

B: どうしてぼくのアイスクリームがこんなにたくさんあるのさ？
G: ビッグサイズのスクープを1つじゃなく2つほしいって，お兄ちゃんが言ったんでしょう。
B: でもこれは多すぎるよ。食べるのにスプーンがなくちゃ。

G: それからナプキンも2, 3枚は必要でしょうね。

お兄さんは何がほしいと言っていますか？
(A) テーブルをふくナプキンを
(B) カップにもっとアイスクリームを
(C) アイスクリームを食べるスプーンを

2. W: Oh no, I ran out of milk for our cookies. Can you ²run to the store and buy milk?
G: I would love to, but I don't know where the store is.
W: It's not too far from here. Just walk to the street corner. It's on the left.
G: ³Are you sure it's on the left side?
W: Of course, you will see the store.

W: どうしよう、クッキーに必要な牛乳が切れちゃったわ。お店に走って行って買ってきてくれる？
G: そうしたいけど、どこにお店があるのか知らないわ。
W: ここからそんなに遠くないわよ。通りの角まで歩いていけば、左側にあるから。
G: 絶対に左側にあるのね？
W: もちろん、左にお店が見えるはずよ。

お店はどこにありますか？
(A) 角の左側に
(B) 角の右側に
(C) 家の左側に

3. M: Welcome to Denny's Restaurant. Would you like a coloring sheet and crayons while you wait for a table?
G: Thank you, I love to color.
M: No problem, waiting is very boring sometimes.
G: Yes, the restaurant looks very busy today.
M: Don't worry. Coloring will make ⁴the time go by fast.
G: I hope so.

M: Denny'sレストランへようこそ。テーブルがご用意できるまで、ぬり絵とクレヨンなどはいかがですか。
G: ありがとう、私ぬり絵は大好きなんです。
M: いいですよ。待ち時間は時には退屈ですからね。
G: ええ、今日はレストランがすごく混んでいるんですね。
M: ご心配なく、ぬり絵をしていればすぐに時間が過ぎますよ。
G: そうですね。

女の子はなぜぬり絵をするのですか？
(A) 時間をつぶすため
(B) 宿題を終わらせるため
(C) ウェイターのお手伝いをするため

4. M: I can't believe it's still ⁵raining outside.
B: I hate rain. I really wanted to play baseball today.
M: Oh wait, I think the sky is clearing up!
B: Awesome. Let's go to the baseball field.
M: ⁶Sounds great, I will get the baseball bat and gloves.

M: 信じられない、まだ外で雨が降っている。
B: 雨なんて大嫌い。今日は野球がしたくてたまらなかったのに。
M: おや、待て、晴れてきたようだぞ！
B: よかった。野球場に行こうよ。
M: そりゃいい。パパはバットとグローブを持って来よう。

お父さんと息子はこれからどこに行くでしょうか？
(A) 美術館に
(B) サッカーの試合に
(C) 野球場に

5. M: Your puppy is just sick. There is nothing to worry about.
B: Oh thank you, I ⁷was scared there was something terribly wrong.
M: You just need to give your puppy a rest and some water to drink.
B: That sounds good. I will surely do that.

M: あなたの犬はちょっと気分が悪いだけですよ。何も心配はいりません。
B: ああ、ありがとうございます。すごく悪いんじゃないかと心配していたんです。
M: しっかり休ませて、水を飲ませてあげればいいでしょう。
B: よかった。必ずそうします。

男の子は何をしようとしていますか？
(A) 獣医さんの助言にしたがう
(B) 犬に薬をあげる
(C) 犬を公園に連れて行く

6. G: This orange juice tastes delicious. Do you want to ⁸try some?
B: No thanks. I am really hungry though. I wish we had some bread and ham.
G: Why do you want bread and ham?
B: I want to make my famous ham sandwich!
G: That sounds better than my orange juice. I am ⁹getting hungry now.

G: このオレンジジュース、おいしいわよ。ちょっと飲んでみる？
B: いや、いらないよ。でもぼくはすごくおなかが空いてるんだ。パンとハムがあったらいいのに。

G: どうしてパンとハムがほしいの？
B: ぼくの特製ハムサンドイッチを作りたいんだよ。
G: 私のオレンジジュースよりよさそうね。私もおなかが空いてきちゃった。

男の子は何をしたいと言っていますか？
(A) オレンジジュースを飲む
(B) サンドイッチを作る
(C) クッキーを焼く

7.
M: Hey, did you by chance see who stole that watch from the shelf?
G: I think so. He looked like an old grandpa with gray hair and big ears.
M: Can you tell my friend what he looked like? She will draw a picture of him.
G: Sure, I can try and remember all the details of what he looked like.
M: Thank you. That would be very helpful in order to [10]solve our case.

M: ねえ君，そこの棚からだれが時計を盗んだのか，たまたま見ていなかったかい？
G: 見たと思います。白髪で耳の大きなおじいちゃんみたいでした。
M: その男がどんなふうに見えたか，私の友達にも教えてくれるかい。彼女がその男の絵を描くから。
G: ええ，やってみます。その人がどんなふうに見えたか，できるだけ詳しく思い出してみます。
M: ありがとう。事件解決に大いに役立つはずだ。

女の子は次に何をするでしょうか？
(A) 男の絵を描く
(B) 男がどんな外見だったかを話す
(C) 盗まれた時計を探す

8.
W: Hello. Would you like to see our kids' menu? The serving sizes are smaller.
B: That's good. I cannot eat [11]as much as my mom and dad.
W: Here is the kids' menu. What would you like to [12]order?
B: I think I will have the grilled cheese sandwich and French fries.
W: Oh really? Our chicken nuggets are the best thing on the kids' menu.
B: But I would like to eat cheese today, and I really like sandwiches.

W: いらっしゃいませ。お子様用のメニューをごらんになりますか？ 小さいサイズのものになります。
B: お願いします。ぼくはママやパパみたいにたくさんは食べられないもの。

W: こちらがお子様用のメニューになります。ご注文は何になさいますか？
B: 焼きチーズサンドイッチとフライドポテトを頼もうと思います。
W: そうですか？ 当店のチキンナゲットは，お子様用メニューで最高のものですよ。
B: でも今日はチーズが食べたいし，ぼくはサンドイッチが大好きだから。

男の子がほしいものは何ですか？
(A) チキンナゲット
(B) たくさんの量の食べ物
(C) 焼きチーズサンドイッチ

Lesson 15

■ 重要ポイント

やってみよう！
soda, the picnic / take an umbrella

■ 練習問題

| 1. (C) | 2. (A) | 3. (B) | 4. (C) |
| 5. (A) | 6. (A) | 7. (B) | 8. (C) |

1. G: Hello, Sam. This is Jenny. It's snowing outside. Why don't we go to the park and make a snowman together? It would be really fun.

   もしもし，サム。ジェニーです。外は雪が降っています。公園に行っていっしょに雪だるまを作らない？ すごく楽しいわよ。

   ジェニーはなぜ電話をしたのですか？
   (A) 面白いゲームを説明するため
   (B) 天気について話すため
   (C) 外に出て遊ぼうとサムを誘うため

2. B: Hi, Carl. It's Jake. I'm having some trouble with my math homework. Can you meet me in front of the library before class tomorrow? I need your help.

   カール，こんにちは。ジェークだ。ちょっと数学の宿題で困っているんだけど，明日，授業が始まる前に図書館の前で会えるかな？ 手伝ってほしいんだ。

   ジェークはなぜ電話をしたのですか？
   (A) カールに手助けを頼むため
   (B) 図書館がどこにあるのかカールに教えてあげるため
   (C) 数学の試験についてカールに教えてあげるため

3. W: Hello, Ji-hu. This is Mrs. Rose, your teacher. Tomorrow, a guest speaker from the zoo is coming to our school. Remember to bring your favorite stuffed animal to class. I'm sure our guest will love to see all the animals.

   もしもし，ジフさん？ あなたの担任のローズです。明日，動物園の方がわが校にお話をしに来られます。あなたの一番好きなぬいぐるみの動物を忘れずに授業に持ってきてください。お客様も動物を全部見たがっているはずです。

   先生はなぜ電話をしたのですか？
   (A) ジフを動物園に招待するため
   (B) ジフにおもちゃを持ってくるように言うため
   (C) 招待した講師について聞くため

4. B: Hi, Luke. It's Ben. My family is going camping this weekend. I can invite a few friends to come. Would you like to go with us? All you need is your sleeping bag. Call me back if you would like to come!

   こんにちは，ルーク。ベンです。今週末に家族でキャンプに行くんだけど，何人か友達を誘ってよいと言われたんだ。君もぼくらといっしょに行かないかい？ 君は寝袋だけ持ってくれば大丈夫だよ。もし来たかったら電話してね！

   ベンはなぜ電話をしたのですか？
   (A) 彼の友達について話をするため
   (B) 寝袋を借りるため
   (C) キャンプに行こうとルークを誘うため

5. W: Hello, Susan. It's your grandmother. I was cleaning my house this morning and found your jacket. I can drop it off at school or I can come to your house later. Call me back and tell me what you want.

   もしもし，スーザン。おばあちゃんよ。今朝家を掃除していたら，あなたの上着を見つけたのよ。学校に届けることもできるし，あなたの家に後で行ってもいいけれど，どっちがいいか電話して知らせておくれ。

   おばあちゃんは何について電話をしたのですか？
   (A) スーザンの上着
   (B) スーザンの学校
   (C) 家の掃除

6. M: Hello, Ryan. This is Mr. Johnson, your teacher. Did you show your reading test paper to your parents? Don't forget to bring it next class. Remember that your parents need to sign it. You don't have reading class with me tomorrow, but if you want, you can put it on my desk.

   ライアン，こんにちは。君の担任のジョンソンです。リーディング試験の答案用紙を君のご両親に見せたかい？ 次の授業に忘れずに持ってくるように。ご両親にサインしてもらうことも忘れないで。明日は私のリーディングの授業はないけれど，もしそうしたければ，私の机の上に置いておいてもいいよ。

   先生がライアンに持ってきてほしいものは何ですか？
   (A) サインをもらった彼の答案用紙
   (B) 彼のリーディングの教科書
   (C) 彼のライティングのプリント

24

7. B: Hi, Kyle. It's John. There is a new playground at the park. I really want to play there. Do you want to go there with me after school tomorrow? I will bring some snacks for us, so we don't get hungry. My mom is baking some cookies now.

やあ，カイル。ジョンだよ。公園に新しい遊び場ができたんだ。ぼくはぜひそこで遊んでみたいんだ。明日の放課後にいっしょに行ってみない？ ぼくがお菓子を持っていくから，おなかが空く心配もないよ。ママが今クッキーを焼いてくれてるんだ。

ジョンはなぜ電話をしたのですか？
(A) おやつを少し持ってきてほしいとカイルに話すため
(B) 公園で遊ぼうとカイルを誘うため
(C) 新しい遊び場について聞くため

8. B: Hey, Paul. It's Scott. I am having a pizza party for my birthday next weekend. Do you think you can come? At the pizza place, there are games we can play and even a rock climbing wall. I know you love to climb. I'm inviting many friends, so I think it will be fun.

ポール，こんにちは。スコットだよ。この週末にぼくの誕生日のためのピザパーティーがあるんだ。君は来られるかい？ ピザのお店にはぼくらが遊べるゲームもあるし，ロッククライミング用の壁もあるんだ。君はクライミングが大好きだよね。たくさん友達を招待するつもりだから，きっと楽しいと思うよ。

スコットはなぜ電話をしたのですか？
(A) ロッククライミングの方法を説明するため
(B) 誕生日パーティーで歌を歌うため
(C) ピザを食べるのにポールを誘うため

■ ミニテスト

| 1. (B) | 2. (C) | 3. (C) | 4. (A) |
| 5. (B) | 6. (A) | 7. (B) | 8. (C) |

1. W: Hi, Kayla. It's Mom. Please ¹remember to water the flowers by the window. Use one cup of water and don't pour it in too fast. Thanks.

こんにちは，カイラ。ママよ。窓際にある花に水をやるのを忘れないでね。カップ1杯ぶんの水をあげて，ただしあまり急いで注がないようにね。ありがとう。

お母さんはなぜ電話をしたのですか？
(A) どこで花を買えばいいのか聞くため
(B) 花に水をあげる方法を説明するため
(C) 窓を掃除するようにカイラに言うため

2. G: Hi, Rachel. This is Gina from music class. I need help playing the new violin song we learned today. Can I ²sit by you tomorrow, so I can ³practice with you?

もしもし，レイチェル。同じ音楽クラスのジーナよ。今日私たちが勉強した新しいバイオリンの曲を弾くのを手伝ってほしいの。あなたといっしょに練習できるように，明日あなたのとなりの席に座ってもいい？

ジーナはなぜ電話をしたのですか？
(A) 新しいバイオリンの曲について話すため
(B) バイオリンを持ってきてくれるようレイチェルに言うため
(C) いっしょに練習しようと頼むため

3. G: Hey, Jane. It's Ashley. I am ⁴calling about our new tennis coach. Do you like him? I think the new coach is kind of mean. But maybe it's because our old coach was so nice. I want to hear ⁵what you think.

もしもし，ジェーン。アシュリーだけど。新しいテニスコーチについて電話したの。あなたはあの人のこと好き？ 私はあの新しいコーチがちょっと嫌なの。でもそう思うのは前のコーチがすごくいい人だったからなのかも。あなたがどう思うのか聞いてみたいわ。

アシュリーは何について電話したのですか？
(A) テニスの練習
(B) すてきな以前のコーチ
(C) 新しいテニスコーチ

4. M: Hello, Billy. This is your teacher, Mr. Smith. The school field trip is next week. You need a permission form from your parents. Please ⁶bring it with you to school tomorrow. If you don't, you can't go on the field trip.

ビリー，こんにちは。担任のスミスだ。学校の遠足が来週にある。保護者に記入してもらう許可書が必要なんだ。明日学校に持ってきてくれ。もし忘れたら遠足には行けないぞ。

先生はなぜ電話をしたのですか？
(A) 学校に許可書を持ってくるようにビリーに言うため
(B) 遠足の行程を説明するため
(C) 学校の予定について話すため

5. G: Hi, Chloe. It's Lucy. Are you tired? I'm really tired now. I think it's because we were working on the art project for so long. By the way, I couldn't find my sketchbook ⁷after I came home. Can you ⁸look around in your room? Please tell me if it's there.

解答・解説 Step 1 25

もしもし，クロエ。ルーシーよ。疲れてる？　私はもうくたくただわ。ずいぶん長い時間，美術の課題に取り組んだからだと思う。ところで家に帰ったら私のスケッチブックが見つからないの。あなたの部屋をちょっと探してみてくれる？　もしあったら教えてね。

ルーシーは何をなくしたのですか？
(A) ランドセル
(B) スケッチブック
(C) 理科の課題

6. M: Hi, Jake. It's your grandfather. I stopped at the store quickly to buy some milk, so you can have milk and cookies ⁹for a snack. When you get to the house, please start doing your homework at the table. I will be back soon.

やあ，ジェーク。おじいちゃんだ。ちょっと店によって牛乳を買ってきた。おやつに牛乳といっしょにクッキーを食べるといい。うちに帰ったら，テーブルで宿題にとりかかるように。すぐに帰るよ。

おじいさんはお店で何を買いましたか？
(A) 牛乳
(B) テーブル
(C) クッキー

7. G: Good morning, Michelle. It's Anna calling. My old friend rides a different school bus than me now because she ¹⁰goes to another school. My mom thinks it's safer if I have a friend to ride the bus with. So can I ride the bus with you, starting today? Do you think that would be OK?

おはよう，ミシェル。アンナよ。私の昔からの友達が，別の学校に行くことになって，別のスクールバスに乗るようになったの。友達といっしょにスクールバスに乗ったほうが安全だってお母さんが言うし，今日からあなたといっしょにバスに乗ってもいいかな？　いいかしら？

アンナがしたいことは何ですか？
(A) 他の学校に通うこと
(B) ミシェルといっしょにバスに乗ること
(C) ミシェルといっしょに歩いて学校に行くこと

8. G: Hello, Stephanie. This is Amy. I called because you left your backpack in the library. But don't worry about it because I'm ¹¹keeping it for you. I have lots of homework to do, so my mom said she can bring it to you. Call me back when you ¹²get home.

ステファニー，こんにちは。エイミーです。あなたがランドセルを図書館に忘れたので電話しました。でも心配しないで，私が保管しているから。私は宿題がたくさんあるから，ママが代わりに持っていくそうです。家に着いたら電話してください。

エイミーはステファニーのために何を保管しているのですか？
(A) 図書館の本
(B) 宿題
(C) ランドセル

Lesson 16

■ 重要ポイント

やってみよう！
eat anything / listening to music

■ 練習問題

1. (A)	2. (B)	3. (C)	4. (A)
5. (A)	6. (C)	7. (A)	8. (C)

1. M: Next week, the second grade class will see a play. Please ask a parent to call your teacher. They need to tell your teacher if you can go or not.

   来週，2年生のクラスが演劇を見学します。親ごさんに，先生に電話するように伝えてください。みなさんが行けるかどうか，先生に伝える必要があります。

   校長先生は何について話していますか？
   (A) 2年生のクラスのための行事
   (B) 保護者の授業参観
   (C) 演目のあらすじ

2. M: Because of the bad weather today, you can go home early. School will end at 1 p.m. The bus will come to pick you up at 1:15 p.m.

   今日は天気がよくないから，早く家に帰っていいです。学校は午後1時に終わります。バスは1時15分に迎えに到着します。

   先生は何について話していますか？
   (A) よく晴れた天気
   (B) 学校が早く終わること
   (C) 保護者に電話すること

3. W: The school dance will be this weekend. Wear your best dancing shoes! We will also have candy and games to play. If you win a game, then you can get a prize. I hope everyone can come and have fun.

   学校のダンスパーティーが今週末に開かれます。あなたの一番のダンスシューズをはいてきてください。キャンディーやゲームも用意しておきます。ゲームに勝てば，賞品ももらえます。みなさんで参加して，楽しんでほしいと思います。

   校長先生は何について話していますか？
   (A) ダンスの仕方を覚えること
   (B) ゲームで勝つ方法
   (C) 学校行事

4. M: The school is having a spelling contest next week. So if you're good at spelling words, please sign up in the main office today. If you win the contest, you get to travel to a big city and try to win the grand prize.

   学校で来週にスペリング大会を行います。単語のつづりに自信がある人は，事務室で本日登録してください。もし大会で優勝すれば，大都市への旅行と，最優秀賞への挑戦権が得られます。

   校長先生は生徒に何をするようにと話していますか？
   (A) 大会に申し込むこと
   (B) 大都市に旅行すること
   (C) 単語のつづりを練習すること

5. M: I just heard thunder in the sky. I think it's going to rain soon. Everyone please pick up all the baseballs and go inside the gym. That is where practice will be today. Once you're inside, start playing catch with a partner.

   たった今，空から雷の音が聞こえましたが，もうすぐ雨になりそうです。全員，野球のボールをすべて拾って，体育館の中に入ってください。今日はそこが練習場です。体育館に入ったらすぐにパートナーとキャッチボールを始めてください。

   野球選手は体育館で何をしなければなりませんか？
   (A) キャッチボールをする
   (B) ランニングの練習をする
   (C) 野球ボールを拾う

6. W: If you were not in class yesterday, you missed the story about the golden lion. Please ask another student which pages to read. Then start reading the story quietly by yourself. After you are finished, get the question paper on my desk.

   昨日の授業に欠席した人は，『金色のライオン』の話を聞き逃してしまっています。他の生徒にどのページを読めばいいか聞いて，各自で黙読してください。終わったら，私の机の上にあるテスト用紙を取りに来てください。

   先生は何について話していますか？
   (A) 『金色のライオン』のあらすじ
   (B) 本の中で読むべきページ
   (C) 昨日の授業内容

7. M: Tomorrow during class, we will go outside to study the flowers that we planted last year. You need a small camera, a notebook, and pencils. We will take photos of the flowers and write down how much they have grown. This is a great way to learn how flowers grow every year.

明日の授業では，昨年私たちが植えた花を観察するために外に出ます。みなさんは小型カメラ，ノートと鉛筆が必要です。花の写真を撮り，どれだけ育ったか記録するのです。これは花が毎年どのように成長するかを知る上で，とてもよい方法です。

先生は生徒たちに何をするように言っていますか？
(A) 授業に必要な道具を持ってくること
(B) 植木鉢の花を描くこと
(C) 外で花を植えること

8. M: I would like to introduce our new player. Welcome to the basketball team, Kevin! Everyone, please have Kevin in every group during practice today. That way he can get to know everyone on the team. Kevin, you can find the practice schedule on the board by the cabinet.

新しい選手を紹介したいと思います。バスケットボールチームへようこそ，ケビン。みなさん，今日の練習では各グループにケビンを入れるようにしてください。そうすればケビンがチームのメンバー全員を知ることができますから。ケビン，練習日程はキャビネット横の掲示板で確認できます。

コーチは何について話していますか？
(A) 練習日程の変更
(B) バスケットボール競技
(C) 新しい部員

■ **ミニテスト**

| 1. (B) | 2. (C) | 3. (A) | 4. (C) |
| 5. (C) | 6. (B) | 7. (C) | 8. (A) |

1. M: On Wednesday, we will have a book fair. At a book fair, you can ¹look at all different kinds of books. And you can buy the books that you like.

水曜日に図書展示会が開かれます。図書展示会ではみなさんはさまざまな種類の本を見ることができます。そして，みなさんが好きな本を買うことができます。

校長先生は何について話していますか？
(A) 図書館の本
(B) 学校の図書展示会

(C) オンラインで本を購入すること

2. W: Please invite your mom, dad, sisters, and brothers to our family fun night this Friday. We will have lots of ²things to do like games, watch movies, and even watch a play!

今週の金曜日に行われる，楽しい家族の夜の集いに，みなさんのお母さん，お父さん，兄弟姉妹の方々を招待しましょう。私たちはゲームをしたり，映画を見たり，さらには演劇を見たりと，たくさんすることがあります。

校長先生は何について話していますか？
(A) 学校の休日
(B) 家族キャンプに行くこと
(C) 家族の夜の集いについて

3. W: We just ordered some new magazines today. If you want to read them, please write your name ³on this paper hanging on the wall. Then I will know ⁴who I should give the magazines to first.

今日は新しい雑誌を何冊か注文しました。読みたい人は，自分の名前を壁に張り出されているこの紙に書いておいてください。そうすればだれに最初に雑誌を渡せばいいのかわかりますから。

生徒たちはどうすれば雑誌を借りることができますか？
(A) 自分の名前を書く
(B) 雑誌を注文する
(C) 司書に話して伝える

4. M: Mary's birthday is tomorrow. She is going to bring cupcakes to ⁵share with everyone. I want each of you to bring your own drink. You could bring juice, milk, or water. We can celebrate Mary's birthday after story time.

明日はメアリーの誕生日です。彼女はみんなに配るためのカップケーキを持ってくる予定です。私はみなさん一人ひとりに自分の飲み物を持ってきてほしいと思います。ジュース，牛乳，水でもいいです。お話の時間が終わったら，私たちはみんなでメアリーの誕生日を祝います。

先生は何について話していますか？
(A) みんなの誕生日
(B) カップケーキの作り方
(C) クラスに飲み物を持ってくること

5. M: I would like to introduce the new runner to our team. This is Sam, and he was the fastest runner at his old school. He ⁶wants to join our track team to meet new friends. So please, ⁷welcome Sam by saying hello

and introducing yourselves.

うちのチームに新しく来たランナーを紹介したいと思う。この生徒はサムといって，彼は以前の学校で一番速いランナーだったそうだ。新しい友達を作るためにわが陸上競技部に加入したいとのことだ。ではあいさつして，一人ずつ自己紹介して，サムを歓迎してやってくれ。

サムはどうして陸上競技部に加入したいのですか？
(A) メダルをもらうため
(B) 外で走るため
(C) 友達を作るため

6. M: Hello everyone. I am the new basketball coach ⁸this year. I started playing basketball 20 years ago. I was a very good player until I broke my ankle last year. I ⁹enjoy teaching basketball to young kids. It is a great sport to play.

みなさん，こんにちは。ぼくは今年のバスケットボールの新しいコーチだ。ぼくは20年前にバスケットボールを始めた。去年足首を骨折するまでは，ぼくはなかなかの選手だったんだよ。若い子どもたちにバスケットボールを教えるのは楽しいことだ。すばらしいスポーツだよ。

コーチは何について話していますか？
(A) 彼のバスケットボールのコーチ
(B) 彼のバスケットボール人生
(C) 彼の子どもたち

7. W: Next Friday is Halloween! To celebrate you can wear a costume to school. For example, you can dress like a witch or a ghost. Your costume can be scary ¹⁰like a monster or funny like a clown. But please, no fake blood. That can get messy, and it might scare some of the other students.

今度の金曜日はハロウィンです！ お祝いのために学校に仮装して来ることができます。たとえば魔女や幽霊のようなかっこうもいいでしょう。衣装は怪物みたいに怖いものでも，ピエロのように楽しいものでもかまいません。でもにせものの血は使わないように。よごれが残ることもありますし，他の生徒たちが怖がるかもしれませんから。

校長先生は何について話していますか？
(A) 怖い話
(B) ハロウィンのパレード
(C) ハロウィンの衣装

8. M: There are many students getting sick these days. I want you to be extra careful, so you don't ¹¹get a cold. Please wash your hands with soap and cover your mouth when you cough. And drink as much water or orange juice as you can. I don't want to see any more students going home in the middle of class because they ¹²do not feel well.

最近病気になる生徒が多くいます。みなさんはかぜにかからないよう特に気をつけてください。石けんで手をよく洗い，せきをするときは口を押さえること。水やオレンジジュースをできるだけたくさん飲んでください。授業の途中で体調を崩して早退する生徒をこれ以上見たくありません。

校長先生は何について話していますか？
(A) 病気を予防する方法
(B) 授業がどれくらい早く終わるか
(C) 学校で暖かく過ごす方法

模擬テスト（第1回）

Reading

1. (B)	2. (A)	3. (C)	4. (A)
5. (B)	6. (C)	7. (C)	8. (B)
9. (B)	10. (A)	11. (A)	12. (B)
13. (C)	14. (B)	15. (C)	16. (B)
17. (B)	18. (C)	19. (A)	20. (B)
21. (B)	22. (C)	23. (B)	24. (C)
25. (A)	26. (B)	27. (A)	28. (C)
29. (C)	30. (B)	31. (B)	32. (C)
33. (C)	34. (A)	35. (B)	36. (B)
37. (C)	38. (A)	39. (B)	

1. (A) オウム
   (B) コウモリ
   (C) ニワトリ

2. (A) どちらのネコも魚を食べている。
   (B) 黒いネコは茶色のネコよりもやせている。
   (C) 茶色のネコは黒いネコよりも太っている。

3. (A) テレビ
   (B) 電話
   (C) カメラ

4. (A) アリ
   (B) 動物
   (C) クモ

5. (A) スカート
   (B) 帽子
   (C) ブラウス

6. (A) 切る
   (B) つかむ
   (C) 洗う

7. (A) くもっている
   (B) 雪が降っている
   (C) 雨が降っている

8. (A) 脱ぐ
   (B) 乗る
   (C) 続ける

9. (A) 冷たい水
   (B) 熱い水（湯）
   (C) 温かい水

10. (A) ハチ
    (B) 鳥
    (C) 板

11. (A) 彼はサンドイッチを食べている。
    (B) 男の子はサンドイッチを食べ終えた。
    (C) 男の子はハンバーガーを食べる。

12. (A) 女の子は友達にささやいている。
    (B) 女の子は電話で話している。
    (C) 女の子は電話を切る。

13. (A) 彼女は大きな本を読む。
    (B) 女の人が新聞を買っている。
    (C) 女の人が新聞を読んでいる。

14. (A) すべて同じ形だ。
    (B) 三角形が一番小さい。
    (C) 円は正方形より大きい。

15. (A) 男の人がポップコーンを食べている。
    (B) 女の人がテレビを見ている。
    (C) 彼はソファーに座っている。

16. (A) テーブルの上にはリンゴが2つある。
    (B) ブドウはこの中で一番大きい。
    (C) オレンジはリンゴの横にある。

17. (A) 彼はとても遅く寝た。
    (B) 男の子は朝早く起きる。
    (C) 今は午前10時だ。

18. (A) 彼女は壁に絵を描いている。
    (B) 女の子は手紙を書くのが好きだ。
    (C) 彼女は絵を描いている。

19. それは場所です。旅行のときに行くところです。ここであなたは飛行機に乗ります。それは＿＿＿＿です。
    (A) 空港
    (B) 駅
    (C) 列車

20. それは甘いものです。食べ物の一種です。真ん中に穴があります。それは何ですか？
    (A) トウモロコシ
    (B) ドーナツ
    (C) タイヤ

21. 逆の意味の言葉は「固い」です。ネコの毛並をさわった感じはこのようです。それはなめらかにも感じられます。それは何ですか？
    (A) 粗い
    (B) やわらかい
    (C) 違う

22. 犬たちは骨を持ってこのような行動をします。人々は宝物を探すときにこのような行動をします。人々は何をするのですか？
    (A) 歌う
    (B) 登る
    (C) 掘る

23. あなたが絵を制作するときにこのような行動をします。ノートにもこのような行動をします。この行動を，色を使ってすることもできます。あなたは何をしますか？
    (A) 拍手する
    (B) 描く
    (C) 持ち上げる

24. みなさんは歴史を見るためにここに行きます。みなさんはここで芸術作品を見ることもあります。そこへ校外見学に行くこともあります。そこはどこですか？
    (A) 公園
    (B) 映画館
    (C) 博物館

25. それは色です。明るい色です。太陽はこのような色に見えます。それはどのような色ですか？
    (A) 黄色
    (B) 青色
    (C) 黒色

26. それは農場にある緑の多い場所です。そこにはトウモロコシがある場合もあります。お米がある場合もあります。そこは何ですか？
    (A) 運動場
    (B) 畑
    (C) プール

27. この日は外がとてもうるさいです。それはおだやかとは言えません。木の葉が風に吹かれています。その日は＿＿＿です。
    (A) 風の強い日
    (B) よく晴れた日
    (C) 涼しい日

[28-31] 招待状を読んで問題28～31に答えなさい。

ハンナ・メイヤーと
ハンナの6年生の友達の卒業パーティーに来てください！

5月25日土曜日午後2時

ハンナの家
29番街210号

出席はキャシー（ハンナの母）まで
701-334-2222番にお知らせください

---

28. あなたはパーティーに参加したいと思っています。あなたは＿＿＿に電話しなければなりません。
    (A) ハンナ
    (B) ハンナのお父さん
    (C) ハンナのお母さん

29. だれのためのパーティーですか？
    (A) ハンナだけ
    (B) ハンナと彼女のお母さん
    (C) ハンナと彼女のクラスメート

30. パーティーはどこで行われますか？
    (A) 学校
    (B) ハンナの家
    (C) レストラン

31. パーティーはいつですか？
    (A) 日曜日
    (B) 土曜日
    (C) 休日

[32-35] ポスターを読んで問題32～35に答えなさい。

Happy Zooに遊びに来てください！

土曜日に来る子どもたちのための
新しいスケジュール

イベント	時間	場所
ライオンの芸を見る	午前11時	ライオンのオリ
サルと写真撮影	午後12時	サルのオリ
ペンギンとお絵かき	午後1時	ペンギンのオリ
イルカショー見学	午後2時	水族館

事務室は月曜日から金曜日
午前9時から午後7時まで開いています

---

32. イベントはいつですか？
    (A) 月曜日
    (B) 金曜日
    (C) 土曜日

33. 何時にイベントは始まりますか？
    (A) 午前9時
    (B) 午後11時
    (C) 午前11時

34. イルカショーを見たければ，あなたは＿＿＿に行けばいいです。
    (A) 水族館
    (B) ペンギンのオリ
    (C) サルのオリ

35. あなたはいつサルと写真を撮ることができますか？
   (A) 午前11時
   (B) 午後12時
   (C) 午後1時

[36-37] 手紙を読んで問題36～37に答えなさい。

> お母さんへ
>
> あなたは世界で最高のコックさんです。お母さんが先週作ってくれたクッキーは本当に最高でした。私はチョコレートチップクッキーが一番気に入りました。クッキーはみんなクラスの友達といっしょに食べました。先生でさえ、もう一度焼いてほしいそうです。みんなが大好きだと言っています。たぶん次はいっしょに焼くことができると思います。私にもおいしいクッキーの作り方を教えてください。
>
> 大好き，
> ターニャ

36. ターニャの望んでいることは何ですか？
   (A) もっとクッキーを食べること
   (B) お母さんといっしょにクッキーを焼くこと
   (C) お母さんにいつもクッキーを焼いてもらうこと

37. 手紙を書いているのはだれですか？
   (A) ターニャのお母さん
   (B) ターニャの先生
   (C) ターニャ

[38-39] 下の文章を読んで問題38～39に答えなさい。

> みなさんは旅行でホテルに泊まったことがありますか？氷のホテルに泊まったことはきっとないでしょう。カナダには氷のホテルがあります。そのホテルの中のものはすべて氷でできていて、冬の間だけ開いています。このホテルですることは、たくさんあります。レストランもあり、氷のカップと氷のお皿から食べることができます。スプーンまで氷です。雪の上で眠ったことはありますか？そう、このホテルでは、氷のベッドの上で眠ることができるのです。

38. これは何についての文章ですか？
   (A) 氷のホテル
   (B) カナダ
   (C) 旅行

39. このホテルにないものは何ですか？
   (A) レストラン
   (B) プール
   (C) 氷のベッド

Listening

1. (B)	2. (C)	3. (A)	4. (B)
5. (A)	6. (A)	7. (B)	8. (B)
9. (A)	10. (B)	11. (A)	12. (C)
13. (B)	14. (C)	15. (B)	16. (A)
17. (B)	18. (A)	19. (C)	20. (B)
21. (A)	22. (A)	23. (C)	24. (B)
25. (C)	26. (C)	27. (A)	28. (B)
29. (C)	30. (B)	31. (A)	32. (B)
33. (A)	34. (C)	35. (B)	36. (C)
37. (A)	38. (B)	39. (C)	40. (B)
41. (A)			

1. My toy bear has big ears.
   私のクマのぬいぐるみは大きな耳をしています。

2. The house is behind a big tree.
   その家は大きな木の後ろにあります。

3. The boy is running after the dog.
   男の子が犬を追って走っています。

4. They are waiting at the bus stop.
   彼らはバス停で待っています。

5. He likes math, but science is his favorite subject.
   彼は数学が好きですが、理科が一番好きな科目です。

6. There are two stars inside a rectangle.
   長方形の中に星が2つあります。

7. The plane took off very smoothly.
   飛行機は順調に飛びたちました。

8. Kim is taller than Ben but is shorter than Jack.
   キムはベンより背が高いですが、ジャックよりは低いです。

9. W: The bell will ring to start class. Please take out your pencils and paper, and put them on your desk.
   もう始業のベルがなります。鉛筆と紙を出して、机の上に置いてください。

10. M: Your homework for today is to read a story and answer five questions about the story.
    今日の宿題は物語を読んでそれに関する5つの問題に答えることです。

11. M: The dog needs to go outside and play. Take the dog out to go and play catch with a ball in the park.
    犬は外に出して遊ばせる必要があります。犬を連れ出して公園でキャッチボールをしなさい。

12. W: The math test is today. Please keep your eyes on your own paper. Do not look at other students' answers.
    数学の試験は今日です。自分の答案用紙だけに目を向けてください。他の生徒の答えを見てはいけません。

13. M: It is not good to cross out words on your paper. Use an eraser when you make a mistake. This is a better way of correcting your writing.
    答案の語句を取り消し線で消すのはよくありません。間違ったら消しゴムを使って消しなさい。書き間違いを直すにはこちらのほうがよい方法です。

14. W: Your mother told me you feel very tired these days. I think it's because you're not getting enough sleep. Try to relax and drink warm milk before bedtime. If you go to bed early, you will feel better.
    あなたが最近とても疲れていると、あなたのお母さんが私に教えてくれました。それはあなたが十分に眠っていないからだと思います。寝る前にはリラックスして温かいミルクを飲んでください。早く眠るようにすれば気分もよくなりますよ。

15. W: Look at your face! It's very dirty. Did you play in the mud? Go to the bathroom and wash your face with soap and dry it with a towel. Dinner will be ready to eat soon.
    顔を見てみなさい。とてもよごれているわ。泥遊びでもしたの？ お風呂場に行って石けんで顔を洗って、タオルで乾くまでふきなさい。もうすぐ夕ご飯のしたくがすむわ。

16. G: OK, let's try riding the bike without my help. If you use both feet to pedal and look straight ahead, you will do fine. I believe that you can do it!
    では、私の助けなしで自転車に乗ってみて。両方の足を使ってペダルをこいで、まっすぐ前を向いていればうまくいくわ。あなたならきっとできるから。

17. M: The school has a new lunchtime rule. When you get your food, please put everything on a tray. The tray will help stop food from being dropped or spilled on the floor.
    学校に新しい昼食時間の規則ができました。料理はすべてトレーの上にとること。トレーを使えば食べ物が床に落ちたりこぼれたりするのを防ぐことができます。

18. W: Flowers need dirt and water to grow. Take your flower seeds and place them underneath the dirt. Then measure one cup of water to pour over the dirt. In one week, the plants should start growing.
    花が成長するためには土と水が必要です。花の種を土の中にうめてください。そしてカップ1杯の水を注いでください。1週間もすれば植物が育ち始めますよ。

19. M: It's time to go to bed soon. I'm going to read you a bedtime story, but first you have to put on your pajamas. The blue colored pajamas are clean, so wear them tonight. Then I will choose a story to read from the bookshelf.
    もう寝る時間だよ。パパが寝る前に童話を読んであげるけど、まずパジャマを着よう。青い色のパジャマが洗い立てだから、今夜はそれを着なさい。そうしたらパパが本棚から本を選んでこよう。

20. B: Can I borrow your book?
    あなたの本を借りてもいいですか？
    (A) Yes, you said that.
    ええ、あなたがそう言ったんです。
    (B) No, I have to use it.
    いいえ、私が使わなければならないので。
    (C) I can't find my book.
    私の本が見つからないんです。

21. W: Are you ready for the test today?
    今日の試験の準備はできた？
    (A) Yes, I think so. ええ、そう思います。
    (B) No, I studied last night.
    いいえ、私は昨日の夜に勉強しました。
    (C) Sure, I can go now. もちろん、もう行けますよ。

22. W: Do you have any questions about the test?
    試験について何か質問はありますか？
    (A) No, I don't. いいえ、ありません。
    (B) Yes, I am nervous. はい、私は緊張しています。
    (C) The test is very hard.
    その試験はとても難しいです。

23. W: Can you please use a red pen to correct the test?
    試験のチェックには赤いペンを使ってくれる？
    (A) Yes, I used a pencil. はい、私は鉛筆を使いました。
    (B) I have many blue pens.
    青いペンならたくさん持っています。
    (C) I'm sorry. I don't have a red pen.
    すみません。赤いペンはありません。

24. W: Can you wash the dishes?
    お皿を洗ってもらえますか？
    (A) Yes, it's right here. はい、ここにあります。
    (B) Yes, that is no problem. ええ、問題ないですよ。
    (C) Yes, I would like that one.
    はい、私はそちらがほしいのですが。

25. W: Please use a towel to dry the dishes.
    お皿をふくのにタオルを使ってください。
    (A) It was good. それはよかった。
    (B) I think it's tomorrow. 明日だと思います。

(C) That's what I'm going to do.
今やろうとしていたところです。

26. W: Did you use soap to wash your hands?
    手をあらうのに石けんを使いましたか？

    (A) No, there were only three.
    いいえ，3つしかありませんでしたよ。

    (B) Yes, I washed the dishes.
    はい，私はお皿をあらいました。

    (C) No, I couldn't find the soap.
    いいえ，石けんが見つかりませんでした。

27. M: What animal do you have in your hand?
    手に持っている動物は何ですか？

    (A) Oh, this is a rabbit. ああ，これはウサギです。

    (B) I left my pet at home.
    ペットを家に置いてきました。

    (C) A rabbit is my favorite animal.
    ウサギは私の大好きな動物です。

28. M: Can I help you carry your rabbit home?
    あなたのウサギを家に運ぶのをお手伝いしましょうか？

    (A) No, I don't like it here.
    いいえ，私はそれがここにあるのが嫌です。

    (B) Sure, that would be very helpful.
    ぜひ，そうしてもらえるととても助かります。

    (C) Yes, there is a store on the corner.
    はい，その角にお店があります。

29. M: Please be very careful when you play with your rabbit.
    ウサギと遊ぶときは十分に気をつけてください。

    (A) Yes, my rabbit is very soft.
    はい，私のウサギはとてもやわらかいです。

    (B) The rabbit loves carrots.
    ウサギはニンジンが大好きです。

    (C) Of course, I will do that. もちろんそうします。

30. G: I think I lost my notebook. I can't find it anywhere.
    B: Did you look inside your desk?
    G: Yes, but it's not in there either.
    B: You should go and look in the library. I bet you left it there.

    G: ノートをなくしちゃったみたい。どこにも見つからないの。
    B: 机の中は見た？
    G: うん，でもそこにもないの。
    B: 図書館に探しに行くべきだよ。きっとそこに置き忘れたんだよ。

女の子は次に何をしますか？

(A) 彼女のお母さんに電話する
(B) 図書館に行く
(C) ノートに書く

31. W: There are too many backpacks on the floor.
    B: What can I do to help you?
    W: Will you grab some off the floor and hang them up on the wall?
    B: Sure, I can do that for you.

    W: 床にランドセルがたくさん置いてあるわね。
    B: 何かお手伝いしましょうか？
    W: いくつか床から拾い上げて壁に掛けてくれる？
    B: わかりました，そうします。

男の子は次に何をしますか？

(A) ランドセルを拾い上げるのを手伝う
(B) ランドセルを外に移す
(C) 家に帰るためにランドセルを背負う

32. M: Our science experiment requires wearing a mask.
    B: Why do we have to wear a mask?
    M: Because it protects you by covering your whole face.
    B: Why does the mask need to cover my face?
    M: So that nothing hot accidently burns your skin.

    M: 私たちの理科の実験ではマスクをつけなければなりません。
    B: なぜマスクをつけなければならないのですか？
    M: 顔全体を覆って守るためですよ。
    B: なぜマスクで顔を覆う必要があるのですか？
    M: 間違って熱いもので皮膚にやけどを負わないためです。

男の子はどのように自分を保護しますか？

(A) 手を使って
(B) マスクをつけて
(C) 目を閉じて

33. W: We need to find you a dress to wear to your cousin's wedding.
    G: Let's go into this store. I think they sell dresses here.
    W: I really like this dress. Will you please try it on?
    G: Mom, it looks wonderful on me. Now I need shoes that match my new dress.
    W: OK, let's go.

    W: あなたのいとこの結婚式に着ていくドレスを探さなくちゃならないわね。
    G: この店に入ってみようよ。ドレスを売っていると思うよ。

W: このドレスがすごく気に入ったわ。試着してみてくれる？
G: ママ，本当にぴったりだわ。次はこの新しいドレスに似合う靴を探さなくちゃ。
W: そうね，行きましょう。

女の子は次にどこへ行きますか？
(A) 靴屋さん
(B) 他のドレスのお店
(C) 彼女のいとこの結婚式

34. W: It's starting to get cold outside. Winter is coming soon!
G: Yes, snow is starting to fall.
W: I love snow. It is very beautiful. Snow reminds me of this lovely winter coat.
G: The white color does look like snow. How much does it cost?
W: It costs $100.
G: Oh, I think I should call my mom and ask. Maybe she will pay for it.

W: 外が寒くなってきたわ。冬ももうすぐね。
G: うん，雪が降り始めたよ。
W: 雪は大好き，とてもきれいだから。雪を見ると，このかわいい冬物のコートを思い出すわ。
G: その白い色は本当に雪みたいね。いくらかしら？
W: 100ドルよ。
G: あら，それならママに電話して聞いてみなくちゃ。ママが払ってくれるかもしれない。

女の子は次に何をしますか？
(A) コートを買う
(B) お金をいくらか借りる
(C) お母さんにお金を頼む

35. M: I am going to schedule an appointment next week to put a cast on your arm. Do you know what a cast is?
G: No, what is a cast for?
M: A cast is like a big bandage for your arm so that it can't move.
G: But I broke my arm, so how does the cast help?
M: It makes your arm stay in the right place. That way, your arm will get better.
G: OK, well I hope it doesn't hurt when you put the cast on me.

M: あなたの腕にギプスをはめるために，来週予約を入れておきましょう。ギプスとは何かご存知ですか？
G: いいえ，ギプスって何のためにするんですか。
M: ギプスは腕につけて腕を動かないようにする，大きな包帯みたいなものです。

G: でも，私は腕を折ってしまったのに，ギプスがどのように役立つのですか？
M: あなたの腕を正しい位置に置いてくれるのです。そうすればあなたの腕も治るでしょう。
G: わかりました，でもギプスをつけるときに痛くないといいな。

女の子はなぜギプスが必要なのですか？
(A) 頭が痛いから
(B) 腕を折ってしまったから
(C) 包帯が必要だから

36. W: Hello, Brian. This is your mother. When school is over, please come home right away. Your cousins want to play with you and are excited to see you.

もしもし，ブライアン，お母さんよ。学校が終わったら家にすぐに帰ってきなさい。あなたのいとこたちがあなたと遊びたがって，あなたと会うのを楽しみにしているわよ。

お母さんはなぜ電話したのですか？
(A) 彼の学校について聞くため
(B) 彼のいとこの家にいっしょに行くため
(C) 放課後に家に帰るようブライアンに言うため

37. B: Hi, Dan. It's Pat. I just got new comic books in the mail today. Would you like to borrow some books? I know you like to read comics.

やあ，ダン。パットだよ。新しいマンガが郵便で届いたところなんだ。何冊か貸そうか？ 君，マンガ好きだろう。

パットは何について電話したのですか？
(A) マンガ本
(B) お笑い
(C) 昔の友達からもらった手紙

38. W: Good afternoon, Marsha. It's your teacher, Mrs. Penny. We have a school trip to the zoo tomorrow. So please pack your own lunch because we'll eat there instead of at school. George will bring juice boxes for everyone to drink.

こんにちは，マーシャ。あなたの担任のペニーです。明日は動物園に遠足に行きます。昼食は学校ではなくそこでとるので，お昼ご飯を持参してください。ジョージはみんなが飲めるように紙パックのジュースを持ってきます。

マーシャは明日何を持っていかなければなりませんか？
(A) カメラ
(B) お昼ご飯
(C) 紙パックのジュース

39. W: There will be no school next Monday because it's a holiday. That means you will have a long weekend and more homework than usual. This will help us finish our book on ocean fish by next week.

来週月曜日は休日なので学校がお休みです。つまり，週末休みが長く，いつもより宿題も多いということです。おかげで海の魚についての本を来週までに読み終えることもできるでしょう。

先生は何をする予定ですか？
(A) 野生動物について話す
(B) 今日，本を読み終える
(C) 追加の宿題を出す

40. M: There will be a big football game after school today. I would like all the students to come and cheer for the team. When classmates are there to watch, the football team always plays better. And today is a very important game to win.

今日の放課後に大きなサッカーの試合がある。私は生徒全員がチームを応援しに来てほしいと思う。クラスメートが観戦しているときには，チームは常によりよいプレーができるものだ。それに今日は，優勝するためにとても重要な試合なんだ。

校長先生は生徒に何をしてほしいと言っていますか？
(A) 試合に出場する
(B) 試合を応援する
(C) 選手に食べ物をあげる

41. G: Hi, Emily. It's Mary. We have a new member in our cello club. She doesn't know anyone yet. So I thought it would be good to help her. Can you ride the bus with her in the morning? She lives pretty close to your house. Just meet her in the morning on the corner.

こんにちは，エミリー。メアリーよ。私たちのチェロ部に新しい部員が入ったの。まだ知り合いがいないから，彼女を助けてあげたいんだけど，朝にいっしょにバスに乗ってくれる？ 彼女，あなたの家のすぐ近くに住んでいるから，朝に角のところで会うといいわ。

メアリーは何について電話したのですか？
(A) バスにいっしょに乗ること
(B) 角にできた新しい家
(C) 新しい部員のかわいさ

模擬テスト（第2回）

Reading

1. (A)	2. (C)	3. (B)	4. (A)
5. (B)	6. (C)	7. (A)	8. (B)
9. (B)	10. (A)	11. (B)	12. (C)
13. (B)	14. (C)	15. (B)	16. (A)
17. (C)	18. (A)	19. (B)	20. (C)
21. (B)	22. (A)	23. (B)	24. (C)
25. (C)	26. (A)	27. (A)	28. (B)
29. (C)	30. (A)	31. (B)	32. (A)
33. (A)	34. (C)	35. (C)	36. (C)
37. (A)	38. (B)	39. (A)	

1. (A) イルカ
   (B) サメ
   (C) タコ

2. (A) 彼女はバイオリンが好きだ。
   (B) 男の子はチェロを弾いている。
   (C) 彼はバイオリンを弾いている。

3. (A) カエル
   (B) アヒル
   (C) 犬

4. (A) 茶色
   (B) 黄色
   (C) 白

5. (A) フォーク
   (B) スプーン
   (C) ナイフ

6. (A) トマト
   (B) タマネギ
   (C) カボチャ

7. (A) 自転車
   (B) 自動車
   (C) タクシー

8. (A) 四角いパイ
   (B) 円いパイ
   (C) 三角形のパイ

9. (A) 満杯の箱
   (B) 空っぽの箱
   (C) 青い箱

10. (A) においをかぐ
    (B) 話す
    (C) 見る

11. (A) 男の子は顔を洗っている。
    (B) 彼は歯を磨いている。
    (C) 彼は水を飲んでいる。

12. (A) 男の子はボールをキャッチしている。
    (B) ボールはへいの上を飛んでいる。
    (C) 彼はボールを投げている。

13. (A) たくさんの木がある。
    (B) 木の下には落ち葉がある。
    (C) 木には葉っぱがたくさんある。

14. (A) 3個のカップはみな同じ大きさだ。
    (B) ピンクのカップは赤いカップのとなりにある。
    (C) 赤いカップが一番小さい。

15. (A) 彼はうなずいている。
    (B) 女の子が首を振っている。
    (C) 彼女は手を振っている。

16. (A) 赤い鉛筆が一番長い。
    (B) 3本の鉛筆がテーブルの上にある。
    (C) 緑の鉛筆は赤い鉛筆より長い。

17. (A) 彼女は台所で料理をしている。
    (B) 彼はポットを使っている。
    (C) その男の人はフライパンを手に持っている。

18. (A) 男の子は科学者になりたい。
    (B) 彼女は科学者だ。
    (C) 彼は看護師になりたい。

19. それは水のある広い場所です。魚が生息しています。陸に囲まれています。それは何ですか？
    (A) 川
    (B) 湖
    (C) 山

20. これはあなたを涼しくします。それはあなたに向かって風をあてます。夏の間に使います。それは何ですか？
    (A) ヒーター
    (B) タオル
    (C) 扇風機

21. これは食べる際に使います。スプーンといっしょに使います。たいてい，金属でできています。それは何ですか。
    (A) 岩
    (B) フォーク
    (C) 棒

22. このような人は強くありません。このような人は重い物を持ち上げることができません。このような人はたいてい非常にやせています。その人は＿＿＿人です。
    (A) 弱い
    (B) 広い
    (C) 心配な

23. これをするためにはペンか鉛筆が必要です。試験の答案用紙に答えを書くときにこうします。紙の上にこれをします。あなたは何をしますか？
    (A) 作る
    (B) 書く
    (C) 着る

24. それはふつう，黄色いものが多いです。子どもたちは学校に行くときに乗ります。それはとても長いです。それは何ですか？
    (A) 自動車
    (B) タクシー
    (C) バス

25. あなたは旅行に行く前にこれをします。あなたは予定表を作るためにこれをします。あなたは＿＿＿を立てます。
    (A) ショッピング
    (B) 物
    (C) 計画

26. 人々は何かを買うときにこれをします。人々はレストランに行ったときにこれをすることもあります。これをするときにお金を渡します。人々は何をしますか？
    (A) 支払う
    (B) 盗む
    (C) 受け取る

27. もしあなたが競走で勝てばあなたはこのような人です。あなたがニワトリを捕まえたければ，このようでなくてはなりません。あなたは遅くありません。あなたは＿＿＿です。
    (A) 速い
    (B) 重い
    (C) おかしい

[28-31] 下の看板を読んで問題28〜31に答えなさい。

```
スーパーモールへようこそ!!
どこに行きたいですか？
A区域
　―フードコート
　―コーヒー店
　―レストラン
B区域
　―衣料品店
　―スポーツ用品
C区域
　―ゲームセンター
　―映画館
```

28. マーリーンはハイキングに行く予定なので靴が必要です。彼女はどこに行けばいいですか？
    (A) A区域
    (B) B区域
    (C) C区域

29. トムは映画を見るために友達と会おうとしています。彼はどこに行けばいいですか？
    (A) A区域
    (B) B区域
    (C) C区域

30. サンディは弟と夕食をとるためにいっしょに来ています。彼女はどこに行けばいいですか？
    (A) A区域
    (B) B区域
    (C) C区域

31. ジョーはシャツとジーンズが必要です。彼はどこに行けばいいですか？
    (A) A区域
    (B) B区域
    (C) C区域

[32-35] 学校の配布資料を読んで問題32〜35に答えなさい。

```
授業参観日の日程表
午前9時      子どもといっしょに登校
午前10時     校長先生の話を聞く
午前11時     全校生徒と昼食
午後12時     学校写真のスライドショーを見る
午後1時      教室へ移動
午後1時30分  先生による授業の見学
午後2時30分  子どもたちと早く家に帰る！
```

32. 行事はどこで行われる予定ですか？
    (A) 学校
    (B) 家
    (C) スポーツセンター

33. いつ昼食をとる予定ですか？
    (A) 午前11時
    (B) 午前12時
    (C) 午後1時

34. だれを対象とした配布物ですか？
    (A) 先生
    (B) 生徒
    (C) 親

35. 行事はいつ終わる予定ですか？
    (A) 午後1時
    (B) 午後1時30分
    (C) 午後2時30分

[36-37] 電子メールを読んで問題36〜37に答えなさい。

```
生徒たちへ

　再度お伝えしますが，歴史のレポートの提出日は今週の金曜日です。金曜日の授業に必ず持ってきてください。金曜日の授業では，みなさんのレポートについてお互いに話し合います。また，私が週末にチェックします。もし提出しない場合は減点します！　だから持ってくることがとても重要です。頑張ってください！

みなさんの担任
シンダーガード
```

36. 先生はなぜ電子メールを書いているのですか？
    (A) 生徒たちに新しい宿題について伝えるため
    (B) 生徒たちに新しい宿題を出すため
    (C) 生徒たちにレポート提出についてもう一度教えるため

37. 宿題の提出日はいつですか？
    (A) 金曜日
    (B) 月曜日
    (C) 週末

[38-39] 下の物語を読んで問題38〜39に答えなさい。

> ジョナサンは夏の旅行について期待をふくらませていました。彼と彼の家族はヨーロッパに行く予定でした。彼らはすべての有名な国に行く予定でした。彼が一番楽しみにしていたのはフランスでした。彼はパリに行ってエッフェル塔を見たいと思っていました。またジョナサンはロンドンに行くのも本当に楽しみにしていました。彼らはビッグベンを見る予定でした。ビッグベンは大きな時計台です。最後に彼の家族はスペイン，イタリア，そしてドイツを見に行く予定でした。それはジョナサンにとってすばらしい旅行になることになっていました。

38. ジョナサンは何を一番楽しみにしていましたか？
    (A) ビッグベン
    (B) エッフェル塔
    (C) スペイン

39. ビッグベンとは何ですか？
    (A) 大きな時計台
    (B) 古いベル
    (C) 高い像

Listening

1. (A)	2. (C)	3. (B)	4. (C)
5. (B)	6. (A)	7. (C)	8. (C)
9. (C)	10. (B)	11. (A)	12. (C)
13. (A)	14. (B)	15. (C)	16. (B)
17. (A)	18. (A)	19. (C)	20. (A)
21. (A)	22. (B)	23. (B)	24. (A)
25. (C)	26. (A)	27. (B)	28. (A)
29. (C)	30. (A)	31. (B)	32. (A)
33. (B)	34. (A)	35. (C)	36. (B)
37. (B)	38. (C)	39. (B)	40. (C)
41. (C)			

1. There is a banana on the table.
   テーブルの上にバナナが1本あります。

2. A cat is chasing a small mouse.
   ネコが1匹の小さなネズミを追いかけています。

3. He catches the ball with one hand.
   彼は片手でボールを捕ります。

4. A lady is cutting in line.
   女の人が列に割り込んでいます。

5. The boy got off the school bus.
   男の子がスクールバスから降りました。

6. He wanted chocolate cake, but his mother gave him apple juice.
   彼はチョコレートケーキがほしかったけれど，お母さんはリンゴジュースをくれました。

7. She came in second in the race.
   彼女は競走で2着になりました。

8. He is not tall enough to get the book from the top shelf.
   彼は本棚の最上段にある本を取れるほど背が高くありません。

9. M: Please go to the main office down the hallway to call your mom.
   廊下の先にある事務室に行ってお母さんに電話してください。

10. W: Today we are going to draw a map. Please open your box of markers and take out three different colors.
    今日は地図を描きます。マーカーペンの箱を開けて異なる色のマーカーを3本取り出してください。

11. M: We are going to go outside for class today. Put on just your hat and jacket. Leave your boots in the classroom.
    今日は野外授業を行います。帽子をかぶりジャケットを着てください。ブーツは教室に置いて行ってください。

12. W: It is not polite to waste food. I would like you to finish eating all the food on your plate. I do not want to throw away perfectly good food in the trash.
    食べ物を捨てるのは失礼なことです。お皿の上の食べ物はすべて食べてほしいと思います。まったく問題のない食べ物をごみ箱に捨てたくはありません。

13. M: You look bored, son. Let's watch a movie on the sofa together. Sit close to me and eat some popcorn. It will be fun.
    退屈そうだね。ソファーに座っていっしょに映画でも見よう。ぼくのとなりに座ってポップコーンを食べなさい。楽しいよ。

14. W: We are now going to take the test. Please remove all of your books and materials off of your desk and place them on the shelf next to the window. All you need for the test is your pencil.
    では試験を始めます。本や資料をすべて机の上から移して窓際の棚にしまってください。試験を受けるのに必要なの

は鉛筆だけです。

15. W: Today we will have a guest speaker, Mr. Jackson. He is a police officer, and he will tell us about his job. It is polite to listen quietly. Only speak by raising your hand when he asks you questions.
今日は特別講師としてジャクソンさんをお招きします。彼は警察官で，自分のお仕事について私たちに話してくださいます。静かに聞きましょう。彼があなたがたに質問したときは必ず手をあげてから話すようにしてください。

16. M: I am going to look at your teeth right now. Please sit back in the chair and open your mouth wide. I am going to use my mirror to see inside your mouth.
これからあなたの歯を診ます。いすに楽に座って口を大きく開けてください。私は鏡を使って口の中を診ます。

17. M: We are going on a field trip to a mountain where many different kinds of plants grow. Once we get there, please take out your plant book and camera to take pictures of the many kinds of plants. I hope you find your favorite one.
私たちはこれからさまざまな種類の植物が生えている山に野外授業に行きます。到着したら植物図鑑とカメラを取り出して，たくさんの種類の植物の写真を撮ってください。皆さんが一番好きな植物を探してほしいと思います。

18. W: Your cup is very dirty. I want you to first rinse the cup with water and then put it in the dishwasher. That way it will be clean and will not collect any germs.
あなたのカップはとてもきたないわね。まず水でカップをすすいでから，皿洗い機の中に入れておきなさい。こうすればきれいになって，ばい菌もつかないから。

19. W: Butterflies are very beautiful creatures. The butterfly can be many different sizes and shapes. I would like you to draw a picture of a butterfly and write the name of all the different parts. This may be on your quiz next week.
チョウはとても美しい生き物です。いろいろな大きさと姿形のチョウがいます。みなさんはチョウを1匹描いて，それぞれの部位に名前を書き込んでください。これは次の週に小テストに出るかもしれません。

20. G: Can I have a pencil?
鉛筆を貸していただけますか？

(A) Yes, you can. いいですよ，どうぞ。
(B) No, I can't see you. いいえ，私にはわかりません。
(C) Thank you. ありがとう。

21. W: Can you please get a book from the bookshelf?
本棚から本を取ってくれる？

(A) OK, I can do that. はい，ぼくがやりましょう。
(B) No, I can't hear you. いいえ，聞こえません。
(C) This book looks strange. この本は変に見えますね。

22. W: Please read the first story in the book.
本の最初の物語を読んでください。

(A) I love the pictures in the book. 私はその本の絵が大好きです。
(B) Can you tell me the page number? ページを教えていただけますか？
(C) Yes, my science teacher taught me. はい，理科の先生から教わりました。

23. W: Do you know what page we are on?
今何ページを見ているかわかりますか？

(A) There are 30 pages. 30ページあります。
(B) Yes, we are on page 12. はい，12ページを見ています。
(C) No, I don't know your name. いいえ，あなたの名前は知りません。

24. M: Where should I put your pillow?
あなたの枕をどこに置こうか？

(A) On my bed please. ベッドの上にお願いします。
(B) I can't help you. あなたを手伝うことはできません。
(C) In the dark. 秘密に。

25. M: What kind of story do you want me to read?
どんなお話を私に読んでほしいんだい？

(A) I will finish reading it soon. もうすぐ読み終わります。
(B) I want to stay up late tonight. 今夜は遅くまで起きていたいの。
(C) I want you to read a funny one. 面白い話を読んでほしいよ。

26. M: OK, it is now time to go to sleep.
さあ，もう寝る時間だ。

(A) But Dad, I'm not tired. でもパパ，まだ疲れてないよ。
(B) Please take my blanket. 毛布を持って行ってください。
(C) I have really good dreams. 本当にいい夢を見るよ。

27. W: Where would you like to sit today?
今日はどこに座りたいの？

(A) Please wait here. ここで待っていてください。

(B) At a big round table. 大きなまるいテーブルに。
(C) I would like spaghetti.
スパゲッティにしようと思う。

28. W: How many people are eating today?
今日は何人で食事するの？
(A) There are five with me. 私を含めて5人です。
(B) There are many people in my family.
私の家族はたくさんいます。
(C) My mom and dad want to eat chicken.
私の両親はチキンを食べたがっています。

29. W: What kind of soup would you like?
スープは何にしますか？
(A) I hate fruit salad. フルーツサラダが嫌いです。
(B) My soup is very hot.
ぼくのスープはとても熱いです。
(C) I would like chicken noodle soup.
チキンヌードルスープにしようと思います。

30. W: You have a very important reading test tomorrow.
G: Yes, I know. I really need to study.
W: I will give you time right now to do so.
G: Really? That would be great, thank you.

W: あなたは明日大事なリーディングのテストがあるんでしょう。
G: ええ、わかってます。本当に勉強しなくちゃならないんです。
W: 今から時間をあげるからそうしなさい。
G: 本当ですか？ それならうれしいです、ありがとう。

女の子は次に何をしますか？
(A) 試験勉強をする
(B) 音楽をちょっと聞く
(C) クラスの友達に話を読んで聞かせる

31. G: The play is next weekend. It is coming up so soon!
B: Oh no, I have to practice more.
G: It is very important that you memorize your lines.
B: I know. I have to memorize them before the play.

G: 演劇発表は次の週末よ。もうすぐだわ！
B: まずいな、もっと練習しなくちゃ。
G: せりふを暗記するのがとても大事なのよ。
B: わかってるよ。発表の前に覚えなくちゃね。

男の子は何をするつもりですか？
(A) 本を読む

(B) 彼のせりふを暗記する
(C) 彼の歌を練習する

32. M: Please turn on your computer, so we can start our lesson.
B: I think my computer is broken.
M: Is your computer plugged in?
B: Ah, no. That seems to solve my problem.
M: Good, now I need you to read the directions, so you can begin your lesson.
B: OK, I will start doing that right away.

M: 授業を始めるために、まずコンピュータの電源を入れてください。
B: ぼくのコンピュータ、こわれているみたいです。
M: ちゃんとプラグは差し込んでありますか？
B: あ、しまった。それでぼくの問題は解決するみたいです。
M: よかった。それでは授業を始めるにあたっての指示事項を読んでください。
B: はい、今そうしようとしているところです。

男の子は次に何をしますか？
(A) 指示事項を読む
(B) コンピュータの電源を入れる
(C) 電源コードのプラグを差し込む

33. G: Happy birthday big brother! I have a big cake for your birthday.
B: Oh great! I love cake!
G: I know you do, but there is one thing you should do. You must wear a birthday hat before you eat your cake.
B: Do I really have to? Hats make my hair messy. But I guess I will wear one today.
G: I'm glad you agreed to do that. While you're wearing it, I'll put candles on the cake.

G: 誕生日おめでとう、お兄ちゃん。お兄ちゃんの誕生日のために大きなケーキを準備したの。
B: うわあ、すごいな。ケーキは大好きだよ。
G: 知ってるわ。でも1つだけお兄ちゃんがしなければならないことがあるわよ。ケーキを食べる前にバースデー帽子をかぶってね。
B: それ、本当にやらなきゃいけないの？ 帽子をかぶったら髪がぼさぼさになっちゃうよ。でもまあ、今日はかぶることにするよ。
G: そうしてくれてうれしいわ。かぶっている間に、ケーキにろうそくをさしておくから。

お兄さんは何をすると言っていますか？
(A) ケーキを切る
(B) バースデー帽子をかぶる

(C) 誕生日のろうそくを吹き消す

34.
W: It is so hot outside today! Can I help you find anything?
G: Well, I need some goggles for swimming lessons. Do you have any in pink?
W: Yes, we have a lot of pink goggles. Would you also like a swimsuit?
G: OK, I will buy a new swimsuit too since my friend is having a pool party next week.
W: Pool parties are always fun to swim at. And you'll have a brand new swimsuit to wear!

W: 今日は外はとても暑いですね。何かお探しですか？
G: あのね、水泳の授業に使う水中メガネが必要なんです。ピンク色のはありますか？
W: ええ、ピンクの水中メガネはたくさん置いてありますよ。水着もいかがですか？
G: はい、水着も買おうと思います。来週友達がプールパーティーを開く予定だから。
W: プールパーティーで泳ぐのはいつだって楽しいですね。しかもあなたは新品の水着を着るのですから。

女の子はなぜ水着を買うのですか？
(A) プールパーティーのため
(B) 友達のため
(C) 水泳の授業のため

35.
M: Welcome. How can I help you today?
B: Well, I need to get my dog's teeth cleaned. They are very dirty and need some care.
M: We can certainly do that for you here. Would you also like your dog's teeth to be whiter?
B: How would his teeth get whiter?
M: There is a special way to whiten your dog's teeth.
B: Maybe next time, I would just like a cleaning today.

M: いらっしゃい、今日はどのようなご相談ですか？
B: ええと、うちの犬の歯をきれいにしたいんです。すごくきたないので、きちんとケアしなくちゃならないと思って。
M: 当院ではもちろん可能です。ついでに歯をもっと白くしましょうか？
B: どうやって歯を白くするんですか？
M: 犬の歯を白くする特別な方法があるんです。
B: それはたぶん、次の機会にします。今日はただきれいにしてほしいんです。

男の子は何をしてほしいのですか？
(A) 犬の歯を白くする
(B) 犬を歯科に連れていく
(C) 犬の歯をきれいにしてもらう

36.
G: Hi, Peter. It's Becky. Would you like to come to my birthday party this weekend? I know you have a baseball game. But I hope you can come and have fun.

元気、ピーター？ ベッキーよ。今度の週末、私の誕生日パーティーに来ない？ 野球の試合があるのは知ってるんだけど、来て楽しんでくれたらうれしいな。

ベッキーはなぜ電話をしたのですか？
(A) 野球をさせてほしいと頼むため
(B) 彼女のパーティーにピーターを招待するため
(C) 幸福な瞬間について話すため

37.
B: Hello, Jill. It's David. I got a bad test score. I want to talk with you about the right answers. I want to know what I did wrong on my test.

もしもし、ジル。デイビッドだ。テストでひどい点数を取っちゃったよ。正しい答えについて君に聞きたいんだ。テストでぼくが何を間違えたのか知りたくてさ。

デイビッドはなぜ電話をしたのですか？
(A) ジルといっしょにテストを受けるため
(B) 正しい答えを聞いてみるため
(C) いっしょに勉強しようとジルを誘うため

38.
M: Hey, it's your father calling. I am running to the store to buy food for dinner tonight. Please let me know what time your violin practice finishes. I will first drive home and then come to pick you up.

もしもし、父さんだよ。今夜の夕食の食べ物を買いにお店に向かっているところだ。バイオリンのレッスンが何時に終わるか教えてくれ。まず家に戻ってから、お前を迎えに行くよ。

お父さんはなぜ電話をしたのですか？
(A) 夕飯のメニューを決めるため
(B) バイオリンの先生について話すため
(C) レッスンの時間を聞いてみるため

39.
W: Congratulations on winning the soccer game last night! Before we practice today, we are going to have a small party. I brought orange juice and bananas for everyone to celebrate. Please relax, have fun, and talk with each other.

昨晩のサッカーの試合での勝利、おめでとう！ 今日は練習する前に小さなパーティーを開こうと思います。お祝いのためにみんなにオレンジジュースとバナナを持ってきま

した。どうかくつろいで，楽しんで，お互いに話をしましょう。

コーチはなぜ食べ物を持ってきたのですか？
(A) お昼ご飯にそれを食べるため
(B) チームの勝利を祝うため
(C) 練習の前にくつろいでもらうため

40. W: If you ate the chicken at lunch today and don't feel well, please come to my office. We think that the chicken got students sick. Some students are saying they have a bad stomachache. Please tell me if you do too.

今日の昼食にチキンを食べて気分が悪くなった人は，私の事務室まで来てください。生徒たちの体調が悪くなったのはチキンのせいだと考えています。ひどい腹痛を訴えている生徒もいます。もしそのようであれば教えてください。

生徒たちはなぜ学校の養護の先生に会いにいかなければならないのですか？
(A) 昼寝をするため
(B) 薬をもらうため
(C) 体調が悪いことを伝えるため

41. M: Hello, Min-ho. This is Mr. Kale, your teacher. A student would like to read the adventure book that you have. Are you finished reading it? If you are, please return it to the school library tomorrow. I know you're busy with your piano lessons. So if you're not finished reading it, bring it next week.

もしもし，ミンホ。あなたの担任のケールです。君の持っている冒険小説を読みたいという生徒がいます。もう読み終わったかな？　もしそうなら，明日学校の図書館に返却してください。ピアノのレッスンで忙しいのは知っているから，もしまだ読み終わってないのなら，来週に持ってきてください。

先生はミンホが何をするように望んでいますか？
(A) ピアノのレッスンをもっと受けること
(B) 生徒に彼の本を渡すこと
(C) 図書館に本を返すこと

ワークブック

Lesson 1

B. Word Study
1. grapes
2. fingers
3. skirt
4. mirror
5. cap

C. Chunk Study
1. on his shoulder
2. a pet rabbit
3. wear a blouse
4. from head to toe
5. a monkey in the tree

Lesson 2

B. Word Study
1. shakes
2. paint
3. warm
4. walk
5. jump

C. Chunk Study
1. standing in line
2. a big smile
3. a round table
4. fast and easy
5. dark brown

Lesson 3

B. Word Study
1. bright
2. kicks
3. ringing
4. orders
5. choose

C. Chunk Study
1. wait for a while
2. ride a bicycle
3. holding his hat
4. sleeping on the bed
5. raise a hand

Lesson 4

B. Word Study
1. clean
2. belt
3. pool
4. triangles
5. happy

C. Chunk Study
1. Heavy school bags
2. too short for you
3. a new building
4. the highest score
5. the same size

Lesson 5

B. Word Study
1. A squid
2. badminton
3. peppers
4. A starfish
5. Cherries

C. Chunk Study
1. Animals like an octopus
2. traditional holidays
3. potato chips
4. bake a carrot cake
5. borrow books

Lesson 6

B. Word Study
1. scary
2. march
3. colorful
4. introduce
5. throw

C. Chunk Study
1. shouted with
2. whispered into
3. traveling around
4. lead the team
5. blow out

Lesson 7

B. Word Study
1. space
2. Beef
3. invited
4. vegetables
5. relay race

C. Chunk Study
1. favorite subject
2. arrive at
3. during recess
4. do jump rope
5. in gym class

Lesson 8

B. Word Study
1. useful
2. vacation
3. forget
4. skateboard
5. board

C. Chunk Study
1. start a fire
2. get some rest
3. can't wait to
4. spin in a circle
5. threw the ball into

Lesson 9

B. Word Study
1. snake
2. sweater
3. candles
4. pet
5. scared

C. Chunk Study
1. instead of
2. win first place
3. a pair of shoes
4. Look at
5. next to me

■ Lesson 10

B. Word Study

1. memorize
2. front
3. hallway
4. meaning
5. toothbrush

C. Chunk Study

1. take a long time
2. calm down
3. come over to my house
4. go for a walk
5. Put on

■ Lesson 11

B. Word Study

1. full
2. decide
3. forward
4. locker
5. trip

C. Chunk Study

1. are, good at
2. on the left
3. sit down
4. right now
5. fell down the stairs

■ Lesson 12

B. Word Study

1. flavor
2. perfect
3. water
4. zipper
5. discount

C. Chunk Study

1. on the radio
2. is worried about
3. a sale on toys
4. look like a princess
5. in a few days

■ Lesson 13

B. Word Study

1. remind
2. ladder
3. tie
4. stack
5. clay

C. Chunk Study

1. put away your toys
2. as soon as possible
3. Hang up your coat
4. get it
5. turned out to be

■ Lesson 14

B. Word Study

1. scoops
2. servings
3. awesome
4. smooth
5. advice

C. Chunk Study

1. a couple of notebooks
2. too far from
3. by chance
4. How come
5. running out of gas

■ Lesson 15

B. Word Study

1. pour
2. tired
3. guest
4. sign
5. different

C. Chunk Study

1. get to
2. lots of people
3. by the way
4. Remember to mail
5. look around the museum

Lesson 16

B. Word Study
1. ankle
2. costume
3. fake
4. cough
5. runner

C. Chunk Study
1. take a photo
2. get a cold
3. For example
4. write down your name
5. share with her classmates

Memo

Memo

はじめての TOEFL Primary® テスト問題集 Step 1